EARTHQUAKE DESIGN CRITERIA

Monograph Series

Engineering Monographs on Earthquake Criteria, Structural Design, and Strong Motion Records

Coordinating Editor, Mihran S. Agbabian

Monographs Available

Reading and Interpreting Strong Motion Accelerograms, by Donald E. Hudson

Dynamics of Structures—A Primer, by Anil K. Chopra

Earthquake Spectra and Design, by Nathan M. Newmark and William J. Hall

Earthquake Design Criteria, by George W. Housner and Paul C. Jennings

EARTHQUAKE DESIGN

CRITERIA

by G. W. Housner

and P. C. Jennings

Division of Engineering and Applied Science
California Institute of Technology

EARTHQUAKE ENGINEERING RESEARCH INSTITUTE

Published by

The Earthquake Engineering Research Institute, whose
objectives are the advancement of the science and practice of earthquake engineering and the solution of national earthquake engineering problems.

This is volume four of a series titled: Engineering Monographs on Earthquake Criteria, Structural Design, and
Strong Motion Records.

The publication of this monograph was supported by a
grant from the *National Science Foundation.*

Library of Congress Catalog Card Number 82-82903
ISBN 0-943198-23-2

This monograph may be obtained from:
    Earthquake Engineering Research Institute
    2620 Telegraph Avenue
    Berkeley, California 94704

FOREWORD

The occurrence of earthquakes poses a hazard to cities that can lead to disaster unless appropriate engineering countermeasures are employed. Recent earthquake disasters with high death tolls, in Guatemala, 1976 (20,000); Iran, 1978 (19,000); Algiers, 1980 (10,000); Italy, 1980 (3,000), demonstrate the great advantages that could be gained by earthquake resistant construction. To provide an adequate degree of safety at an affordable cost requires a high level of expertise in earthquake engineering and this in turn requires an extensive knowledge of the properties of strong earthquakes and of the dynamics of structures that are excited by ground shaking. To achieve this it is necessary for relevant information to be published in an appropriate form.

This monograph by G. W. Housner and P. C. Jennings is the fourth in a projected series of monographs on different aspects of earthquake engineering. The monographs are authored by experts especially qualified to prepare expositions of the subjects, and each monograph covers a single topic with more thorough treatment than would be given to it in a textbook on earthquake engineering.

The monograph series grew out of the seminars on earthquake engineering that were organized by the Earthquake Engineering Research Institute and were presented in Los Angeles, San Francisco, Washington D.C., Seattle, Chicago, Mayaguez, P.R., St. Louis, and Houston, and were aimed at acquainting engineers, building officials, and members of government agencies with the basics of earthquake engineering. In the course of these seminars it became apparent that a more detailed written presentation of each seminar topic would be of value to the members of the audience, and this led to the monograph project. The seminar presented by Dr. Housner and that presented by Dr. Jennings have been combined in this monograph on design criteria, which presents information on the earthquake performance of structures and on important aspects of specifying seismic design criteria. The first three monographs in this

5

series provide background information that will be helpful to the reader of this monograph. The opinions expressed in this monograph are those of the authors and are not necessarily those of the Earthquake Engineering Research Institute or the National Science Foundation.

The EERI monograph project, and also the seminar series, were funded by the National Science Foundation. EERI member M. S. Agbabian served as Coordinator of the seminar series and is also serving as Coordinator of the monograph project. Technical editor for the series is J. W. Athey. Each monograph is reviewed by the members of the Monograph Committee: M. S. Agbabian, G. V. Berg, R. W. Clough, H. J. Degenkolb, G. W. Housner, and C. W. Pinkham, with the objective of maintaining a high standard of presentation.

Monograph Committee
September, 1982

PREFACE

An earthquake disaster, from the engineering point of view, is a situation in which the intensity of ground shaking produces stresses and strains that exceed the strengths of the structures. Therefore, when the design of a project in a seismic region is planned, the specification of the earthquake resistance is a key element to prevent failure or excessive damage in the event of an earthquake. If it were possible to predict precisely the ground motions that will occur at the site during the lifetime of the project, then a corresponding design could be made; unfortunately, it is not possible to predict precisely future ground motions and this causes special problems. An earthquake hazard assessment that identifies past earthquakes that have occurred in the region, relevant recordings of strong ground shaking, potentially active faults, etc., can provide an idea of what might be expected in the future, though this can only be quantified in a probabilistic sense. The question, then, is: Given the probability of future ground shaking, what level of earthquake resistance should a structure have? The correct decision will depend upon the cost of providing earthquake resistance, the cost of repairing future damage, the consequences of failure, etc., so that different decisions will be appropriate for different situations. The formulation of earthquake design criteria for a major project embodies decisions about the earthquake resistance that should be given to its various elements.

The question of appropriate earthquake resistance does not usually arise in the design of ordinary buildings that are governed by the prevailing code. It should be recognized that the building code is a simplified form of design criteria that specify the strength that structures should have but does not take into account all of the relevant items. For example, the code does not take into account in a precise manner such things as: the earthquake hazard at an actual site; the fact that different buildings may have different amounts of damping which will affect earthquake response; the actual vibratory motion of

Failure of a massive reinforced concrete column supporting a freeway overpass bridge during the February 9, 1971 San Fernando, California earthquake. The column suffered a shattering failure caused by a combination of large shearing force and inadequate shear reinforcement.

a structure during an earthquake; the actual ductility that structures have and its effect on earthquake performance. It is desirable, therefore, that engineering judgment be used when designing under code requirements, and for this a knowledge of earthquake design criteria will be helpful.

To set the earthquake design criteria for a major project is not a simple matter, for many factors must be considered and judgment must be exercised. This monograph presents relevant features of the earthquake problem, leading to an overview of earthquake-resistant design and the function of design criteria. The uses of seismological and geological data and the way structures respond to strong ground motions are discussed, in order to understand the formulation and the limitations of appropriate engineering design criteria. Using this information, we then discuss earthquake design criteria in terms of design spectrum, damping values, and ductility; the uses of accelerograms and artificial earthquake records; and the role of statistical and probabilistic analyses. Aspects of review committee procedures and the desired design conservatism are also important elements in arriving at the final set of design criteria. The first appendix provides case studies on the recorded responses of two buildings and shows how important engineering information about the performance of a structure can be deduced in a relatively simple manner. The second appendix reproduces the seismic requirements of the Uniform Building Code as an example of simplified design criteria that do not take into account explicitly all of the important factors.

Structures responding to earthquake ground shaking deform in a highly complex way and the design of structures to survive as desired is not a simple problem. Earthquake engineers need a broad knowledge and a thorough understanding of all the facets of the problem.

George W. Housner
Paul C. Jennings
California Institute of Technology

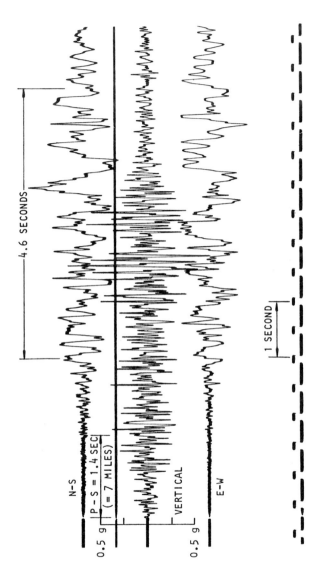

Accelerogram recorded near the causative fault of the M5.7 Westmorland earthquake of April 26, 1981. This shock centered 15 miles northwest of El Centro, California and was on the same fault system as the M6.5 Imperial Valley earthquake of October 15, 1979. The strong phase of shaking had a duration of approximately 3.5 seconds. The vertical motion (P wave) triggered the instrument and then was followed by the horizontal motion (S wave). The vertical motion had higher frequencies than the horizontal, which is typical.

CONTENTS

Figure 1. School building that collapsed during the March 10, 1933 Long Beach earthquake. This M6.2 earthquake originated on a fault that passed through the city. This earthquake provided the first strong motion accelerograph record, which showed peak accelerations of approximately 0.30 g. Many unreinforced brick buildings were severely damaged; in particular, many school buildings were dangerously damaged. This earthquake was the cause of effective seismic design requirements first being included in the U.S. building codes.

Earthquake Design Criteria

INTRODUCTION

The design of structures and facilities to resist earthquakes poses problems that differ from those encountered in the design for ordinary loads. Normal operational loads occur frequently over the lifetimes of structures, and experience therefore accumulates quickly. Because of this, building codes and other standards of practice evolve rapidly to deal successfully with loads of this type. Because such loads may occur many times, or constantly, during the lifetime of the structure, the induced stresses and strains must be well below the limits of the materials involved.

In contrast, even in the most seismic areas of the world the occurrence of very strong shaking at a given site is a rare event. Most structures complete their useful lifetimes without being subjected to the intense shaking that can occur in the central region of a major earthquake. The infrequent occurrence of severe loading influences the process of earthquake-resistant design. First, the infrequency of strong earthquakes has tended to foster the attitude that the problem could simply be ignored. Seismic provisions in building codes, the measurement of strong ground motion, and research in earthquake engineering were begun only in the twentieth century, even though construction is one of mankind's oldest technologies and earthquake damage is reported in the earliest historical records. In the United States, earthquake-resistant design provisions were not included in the main body of the building codes until 1933, the year of the Long Beach earthquake, when Los Angeles adopted a requirement that structures be designed for 0.08 g. Second, the experience in earthquake-resistant design accumulates slowly. For example, in this century San Francisco has experienced only one strong earthquake, the disastrous shock of 1906, and portions of the Los Angeles area have received strong shaking only in 1933 or during the San Fernando earthquake of February, 1971. This means that the planning of programs to measure ground shaking and structural response must be very far-sighted, and it also means that most designers will design many structures or facilities before any of their designs are really tested by strong earthquake motions.

Under these circumstances it is essential to study and learn from the occurrence of damage in past earthquakes, as well as to thoroughly investigate damaging earthquakes wherever they might occur in the future. Finally, the rarity of truly strong shaking at a site implies that such forces need not be resisted within the elastic limit of the materials of construction. It is not economical to design every structure to resist the strongest possible earthquake without damage, since most structures will never experience such shaking. The philosophy implicit in modern building codes, which are design criteria, is to resist moderate shaking without damage, but to permit yielding and structural damage in the event of very strong shaking, provided the damage is not unduly hazardous to life and limb. Thus, for strong shaking, building codes are designed to protect the occupants, not the owner's investment. Similar design philosophies have evolved for other rare but extreme loads, for example, those from high winds. For critical structures such as dams, nuclear power plants, long-span bridges, etc., the design philosophy is more conservative, and special consideration is given to the seismic design criteria.

Most buildings are designed in accordance with the building code, and this relieves the engineer from the necessity of making judgmental decisions about the appropriate strength of the structure, the ductility it should have, etc. The building code, in effect, represents a consensus of how ordinary buildings should be designed. On the other hand, when special projects are to be designed to resist earthquake motion, problems arise which are not encountered in the design of ordinary buildings. There can be major weaknesses in the design if the building code is applied to structures whose dynamic properties differ markedly from those of ordinary buildings. Special structures require special consideration: because of cost, potential hazard, or the need to maintain function, or because of special materials of construction. For example, specific attention should be given to how the special structures or facilities will perform during future earthquakes: what is acceptable infrequent damage; how much

14

should be invested in providing earthquake resistance; will the design be approved by an outside review? Such questions are certain to arise when designing high-rise buildings, dams, nuclear power plants, long-span bridges, oil refineries, LNG (liquefied natural gas) storage facilities, offshore drilling platforms, chemical process facilities, port and harbor facilities, and other similarly complex and costly installations. It is very important that appropriate earthquake engineering decisions be made for such projects, from the standpoints of both safety and cost. These decisions are most effectively made by the project engineer, as he is responsible for the engineering design and he and his staff are in the best position to have an overall view of the project. Although these decisions are sometimes made jointly by the involved parties, the project engineer should take a leading role; it is improper to permit the decisions regarding design criteria to be made solely by the owner, by the consultants, or by the architect, for they will usually lack the knowledge and experience that is required.

The Problems of Earthquake-Resistant Design

In the earthquake-resistant design of major projects, two types of problems are encountered. The first are problems of a purely technical nature, which include the determination of the desired strength of the structure, the choice of structural type and material, the methods for framing and connections, the allowable stresses and strains, and the many details that comprise the engineering design process from its inception to the final structure or facility. The second kind of problem is more managerial in nature; these include the coordination of the contributions of consultants, such as geologists, seismologists, earthquake engineers and geotechnical engineers, and the presentation and defense of the project and its earthquake-resistant design before various governmental bodies and regulatory agencies, including the preparation of required documentation and backup material. The second type of problem was at one time relatively unimportant, but in recent years the activity in this area has increased greatly and some large projects now have numerous consultants and must receive approval from fifty or

15

more different political or regulatory bodies. A sizeable fraction of the attention of senior professionals is devoted to this aspect of the project; and in some instances it seems to assume even greater importance for the success of the project than does the engineering design itself.

The first, and perhaps the most difficult, technical problem in the earthquake-resistant design of a major project is the formulation of the design criteria, although the subsequent engineering analysis and design may also be difficult and are critical to the successful completion of the project. When formulating the design criteria it is necessary to keep in mind that, fundamentally, they are a means of specifying the desired earthquake resistant capability of the structures and facilities. The objectives of the criteria are twofold: First, to provide levels of earthquake resistance for the various parts of the project that are consistent relative to each other; and, second, to provide a level of earthquake resistance that is appropriate to the desired performance of the facility.

On the non-technical side, the requirements of coordinating the technical specialists and the involvement with regulatory agencies and political bodies can place a heavy burden on the project manager and his staff. In order to do his job effectively, the project manager must ensure good communication between the consultants and the designers; that is, between those who contribute information upon which the design criteria are based and those who will utilize this information. In the past, difficulties have sometimes arisen because of misunderstandings, particularly between engineers and geoscientists whose training and experience predispose them to look at the earthquake problem differently. It is also essential for the project manager to have a good overall grasp of the various aspects of the earthquake design problem, for he must assess the degree of conservatism in the final design and must arrange efficient interaction with regulatory and political groups.

Function of the Design Criteria

The primary function of design criteria in general, and earthquake-resistant design criteria in particular, is to restate a complex problem that has unknowns and uncertainties, into an unambiguous, simplified form having no uncertainties. The design criteria should provide clearly stated guidelines for the designers. For example, when actually designing a structure, an engineer needs to know the forces and deformations that the structure should be able to resist. Some of these forces, such as dead loads imposed by gravity, are well known, but others that result from transient actions of nature or man, such as earthquake, wind or live loads, are not known. This lack of knowledge must somehow be circumvented and a precise, unambiguous statement of the design conditions must be given to the design engineer. This is accomplished by means of the design criteria. The designer also needs to know the properties of the materials and structural elements that will be used, but as these are not precisely known, mainly because of imperfections in materials and workmanship, the design criteria must also take this into account. In the preparation of the design criteria, allowance must be made for the uncertainties, and it is necessary to be cognizant of all the unknowns for which allowances must be made.

The traditional engineering design criteria, for example those in the Uniform Building Code, specify live loads that are greater than the actual loads typically encountered, and specify allowable design stresses that are appreciably less than the expected ultimate strength of the material. The purpose of this procedure is to ensure extra strength that is sufficient for unforeseen variations in loads, in material properties, and in workmanship. These criteria, in effect, tell the design engineer: "if you design according to these requirements, the structure will be considered adequate." A similar approach could be taken for earthquake-resistant design if the conditions were more or less the same for all projects. However, because the seismic hazard varies markedly from place to place and because structures and facilities vary in importance, cost, length of life, ease of repair, materials of construction and consequences of failure, the formulation of seismic design criteria for other than ordinary buildings cannot, in general, be codified simply; special knowledge and judgment are required for formulating the criteria.

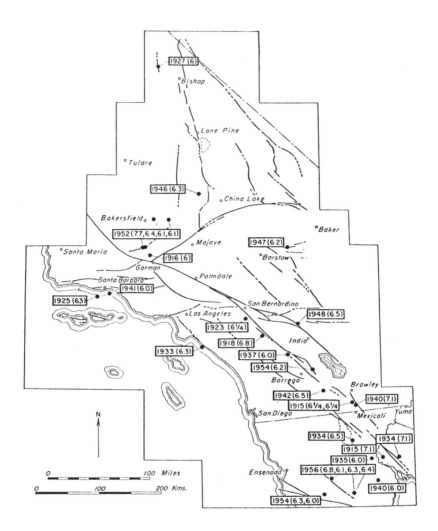

Figure 2. Earthquakes of magnitude 6.0 or greater occurring in the southern California seismic region during a 50-year period (1913–1963). Earthquakes of magnitude 6.0 are potentially damaging to structures close to the causative fault. This plot of earthquakes gives an idea of the earthquake problem, but it should be remembered that the distribution of earthquakes during the next 50 years can be expected to differ from that of the preceding 50 years. (Ref. 1)

18

The Use of Seismological
and Geological Data

When designing structures for a seismic region, what the engineer would really like to know is the strongest ground shaking that the site under consideration will experience during the lifetime of the planned facility. This pre-knowledge, however, is not available, so recourse must be had to estimating what might happen in the future by studying what has happened in the past. Seismological and geological data form the basis for estimating future ground motions, including shaking and possible fault rupture, and studies for important facilities sited where the possibility of major earthquakes must be considered nearly always involve geologists and seismologists.

The seismic history of a region in the U.S. shows what has happened in the recent past, for example the last two hundred years, and thereby gives an indication of what might be expected in the next two hundred years. In a similar way, geological studies can give information on the occurrence of faulting and earthquakes over a longer time span, typically thousands or hundreds of thousands of years, and can thereby provide longer term estimates of the activity of faults than is available from the historical record alone. In this sense the past is used by the geologists and seismologists to predict the future. The results of their studies are often given to the earthquake engineering consultant or to the project manager by statements such as: The design earthquake should be a magnitude M earthquake on the F fault with recurrence interval of Y years, or: The earthquake hazard is represented by a magnitude M earthquake within 25 miles of the site, with probability P of occurrence during a 100 year interval. The reliability of such information depends on the quantity and quality of the data available to the geoscientists. The correct use of the recommendations by the earthquake engineers and the project manager requires an understanding of the terminology and concepts used by the scientists.

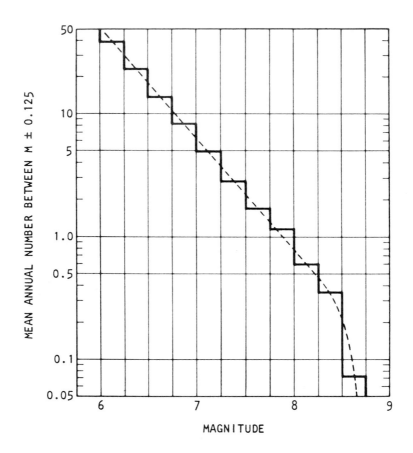

Figure 3. Expected number of world earthquakes per year. The bar graph gives the expected number of shocks between M7.0 and M7.25, and between M7.25 and M7.50, etc. When plotted on log paper, the data fit a straight line except at magnitudes greater than 8.5. This is a statistical indication that there is an upper bound for size of earthquakes. The occurrence of earthquakes in California plot to fit a similar truncated straight-line distribution, though the numbers for the 150,000-square-mile area are smaller. To represent the 100,000-square-mile southern California seismic region shown in Figure 2, the world earthquakes should be divided by 150. (Ref. 4)

Earthquake Magnitude

Any measurement that characterizes the size of the area of strong shaking, or the extent of the "felt area," or the total energy released in shaking, could serve as an indication of the size of the earthquake. As originally developed by C. F. Richter at the California Institute of Technology, the earthquake magnitude scale uses as the pertinent measurement the peak amplitude recorded by a standard Wood-Anderson seismograph, which has a natural period of 0.8 seconds, approximately 80% of critical damping and a magnification of 2800.* The peak amplitude, A, of Wood-Anderson seismograms varies over the surface of the ground in a manner similar to the variation of intensity of ground shaking, being very small at large distances from the fault and thousands of times larger close to the fault; so for a measure, the $\log_{10}A$ is used. A schematic plot of $\log_{10}A$ for an earthquake is shown in the accompanying diagram (Fig. 4) where it is seen that the contour lines of constant values are rather irregular oblong curves. The plot of $\log_{10}A$ forms a hill-shaped surface and it is clear that the volume of the hill would be a good measure of the size of an earthquake, but it would be impractical to evaluate. A less precise, but more practical, measure is that defined by Richter:

$$M_L = \log_{10}A - \log_{10}A_0(\Delta)$$

In this expression, M_L is the local magnitude, Δ is the epicentral distance in kilometers, and $A_0(\Delta)$ is the Wood-Anderson amplitude corresponding to an earthquake with magnitude zero. The variation of $A_0(\Delta)$ with distance was determined from data and the level was fixed by setting its value at 10^{-3} millimeters for a distance of 100 km (Ref. 10).

Actually, most seismographs are not Wood-Anderson instruments, so seismologists must account for instrumental characteristics, as well as distance, in determining local magnitude.

---

* This instrument can be compared with the standard seismoscope which has a natural period of 0.75 seconds and 10% of critical damping, and can also be used for magnitude determinations.

Because of the noncircular shape of the contour lines of $\log_{10}A$, two different seismographic stations will not, in general, compute the same value of M_L, and the "official" value is usually the weighted average from several records. Also, the magnification of the standard Wood-Anderson instrument and of almost all other seismographs is such that the instruments are driven off-scale by motion strong enough to be felt, so the use of seismographs to determine the magnitudes of larger earthquakes necessarily requires the readings to be made at large distances where the character of the ground motion is much different from that near the fault. At such distances, the motion does not contain direct information about the nature of the close-in, potentially destructive shaking. To help correct for this deficiency, recent studies have used the recordings from strong-motion accelerographs to compute the response of a standard

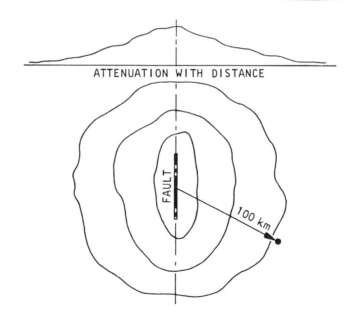

Figure 4. A schematic plot of the value of $\log(A/A_0)$ for an earthquake, where A is the amplitude of a Wood-Anderson seismogram. The value decreases with distance from the fault, and the contour lines of equal values are irregular in shape. The plot forms a hill, and the volume under the hill would be a good measure of the size of the earthquake. The Richter magnitude is based on the value of amplitude A at 100 km.

Wood-Anderson seismograph. These synthetic seismograms are then used to calculate the local magnitude, M_L. When local magnitudes are used to define the ground motion to be considered in the design of structures, it is obviously preferable to base the magnitude on recordings of strong ground motion rather than on more distant, much weaker and more dispersed motions. For example, the intensity of shaking close to the center of a causative fault having 60 miles length of slip would be little different from the intensity near the center of a 400 mile long slip, whereas a sensitive seismograph 10,000 miles from the fault would record markedly different intensities.

Seismic waves change their character as they travel away from the causative fault. In particular, at larger distances the compression waves, shear waves and surface waves separate out and the nature of the waves also change. This has led to certain refinements in determining earthquake magnitudes, and other magnitude scales have come into use. The most common of these are the surface-wave magnitude M_s, the body-wave magnitude m_b, and the moment magnitude M_w. In general, the different magnitude scales do not give the same numerical values, although they agree at some levels and there are empirical techniques for converting from one to another. At distances of a thousand kilometers and more, surface waves of 20-second period predominate in observed seismograms and the amplitude of this motion is used to determine M_s, which is the value most commonly reported in the press for major earthquakes. Earthquakes smaller than about $M_L = 6$ typically do not generate enough surface waves for a determination, so the M_s scale is designed to agree with M_L for magnitudes in the range of 6 to 6½. For larger earthquakes the value of M_s consistently exceeds that of M_L. For example, the 1906 San Francisco earthquake had the approximate magnitudes $M_s \approx 8.3$ and $M_L \approx 6.9$. The largest observed local magnitudes are in the 7–7¼ range, whereas surface wave magnitudes as high as 8.6 have been assigned.

For the very largest earthquakes in history, such as the Chilean earthquake of 1960 and the Alaskan earthquake of 1964, the surface-wave magnitude "saturates" in the sense that it cannot well distinguish two very large events of different fault lengths on the basis of the maximum amplitude of the 20–sec surface waves. For this reason H. Kanamori developed the moment magnitude M_w. This magnitude scale is based on the total elastic strain energy released by the fault rupture, and this is related to the seismic moment M_o defined by

$$M_o = \mu A \bar{D}$$

in which μ is the modulus of rigidity of the rock (commonly denoted by G in the engineering literature), A is the area of the rupture surface of the fault and $\bar{D}$ is the average fault displacement. M_o can be estimated from geological evidence which defines the area and extent of rupture, or from records of long period seismographs at large distances, for which even the largest earthquake appears to be a relatively short event. Because M_w and M_o do not saturate and do measure all the energy released, even that at periods of tens and hundreds of seconds, they are of more fundamental scientific interest to seismologists than the local magnitude, M_L. However, M_w and M_o are not as numerically precise as M_L and their relation to the nature of potentially damaging strong ground motion is necessarily much more tenuous than that of M_L. The largest earthquake on the moment magnitude scale is the Chilean event of 1960 which had a fault length of approximately 600 miles and an assigned value of $M_w = 9.9$, compared to $M_s = 8.6$; the 1906 San Francisco earthquake had a fault length of approximately 200 miles and, as noted, $M_s \approx 8.3$.

Having these different magnitudes introduces an element of confusion into earthquake engineering. The most commonly used magnitudes, as given in Gutenberg and Richter's *Seismicity of the Earth* (Ref. 4) or in the U.S.G.S. publication *United States Earthquakes* (Ref. 15), are M_L for moderately large earthquakes (M = 6.4 for 1971 San Fernando) and M_s for large earthquakes (M = 8.4 for 1964 Alaska), and the consistent use of M in this way means that its value will convey an idea of the size of the event. Because practices vary, it would be advisable to ascertain what magnitude scales are used in any presentation concerning magnitudes.

The body-wave magnitude, m_b, is determined from waves of

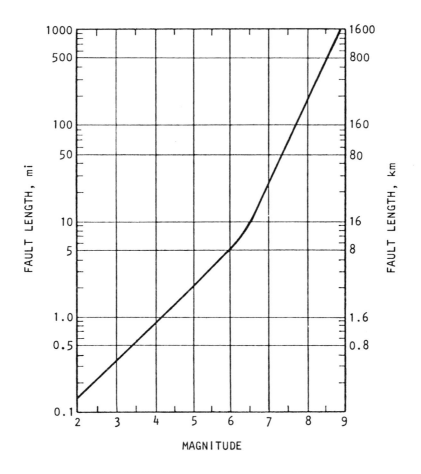

Figure 5. Idealized curve showing the approximate relation between the magnitude of the earthquake and the length of the fault rupture. For example, for the M8¼ San Francisco earthquake of 1906, the graph gives approximately 250 miles for the length of fault slip, and this agrees with the observed length. For the M6.5 San Fernando earthquake of 1971, the graph gives 10 miles, which is in good agreement with the length inferred after the earthquake. The graph is based on the assumption that for magnitudes equal or less than M6 the slipped fault area is approximately circular in shape, although this is sometimes not true for real earthquakes. For large magnitudes the length of fault slip is large but the vertical dimension of fault slip is assumed not to exceed approximately 10 miles.

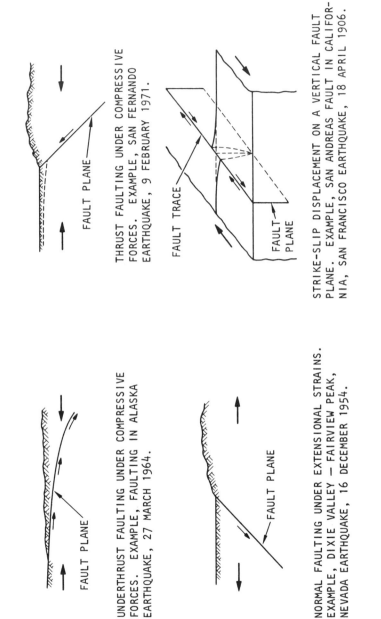

THRUST FAULTING UNDER COMPRESSIVE FORCES. EXAMPLE, SAN FERNANDO EARTHQUAKE, 9 FEBRUARY 1971.

FAULT PLANE

STRIKE-SLIP DISPLACEMENT ON A VERTICAL FAULT PLANE. EXAMPLE, SAN ANDREAS FAULT IN CALIFORNIA, SAN FRANCISCO EARTHQUAKE, 18 APRIL 1906.

FAULT TRACE

FAULT PLANE

UNDERTHRUST FAULTING UNDER COMPRESSIVE FORCES. EXAMPLE, FAULTING IN ALASKA EARTHQUAKE, 27 MARCH 1964.

FAULT PLANE

NORMAL FAULTING UNDER EXTENSIONAL STRAINS. EXAMPLE, DIXIE VALLEY — FAIRVIEW PEAK, NEVADA EARTHQUAKE, 16 DECEMBER 1954.

FAULT PLANE

Figure 6. Four different types of faulting that generate earthquakes. Close to the fault, the type of faulting can have a significant influence on the ground shaking, but at greater distances the influence is small. In actual earthquakes there may also be a component of displacement perpendicular to that shown in the diagram.

26

about one-second period that occur in the early part (P-wave) of distant seismograms. It is useful, for example, in assessing the size of large, deep-focus earthquakes, which do not generate strong surface waves.

Seismological Data

Depending on the region, seismological data are available in various amounts and degrees of quality. There are countries with some form of seismic record going back as much as two or three thousand years, while the historical record in the western United States is seldom as long as two hundred years. Instrumental seismology has, of course, a much shorter history, with a maximum of about one hundred years. Similarly, there are some regions having networks of seismic instruments sufficiently good to record all perceptible shocks and to determine their locations to within a few kilometers; however, most seismic regions have much less extensive coverage. Seismological data of high quality implies instrumentally determined magnitudes and epicenters of all significant events, with locations accurate enough to correlate earthquakes with geologic features of the region. Earthquake data must include a sufficiently large number of events so that enough earthquakes of larger magnitudes are present to characterize events that must be considered in the design.

In practice, the size of an earthquake is described by the extent of faulting or by its assigned magnitude (or magnitudes) as determined from the amplitudes of seismic waves radiated by the earthquake. When a fault ruptures, there is a sudden reduction of shear stress (stress-drop) at the fault plane which transforms static strain energy in the rock into dynamic stress waves. As the stress waves travel away from the fault they produce shaking of the ground surface whose intensity attenuates with increasing distance. The waves are complex, taking different forms and traveling at different speeds; they include compressive waves, shear waves, Rayleigh waves, Love waves, etc., as well as reflected and refracted components. These waves approach a site on the surface of the ground from different directions, both in azimuth and in elevation, with the predominant transport of

27

Figure 7. Aerial view of a portion of the San Andreas fault that is southeast of Los Angeles. The camera view is looking northwest toward Los Angeles. The left side of the fault is part of the Pacific Ocean crustal plate whose main body is moving toward the Aleutian Islands at a rate of approximately 1.5 inches per year. This buildup of shear strain causes episodic stress failures on the fault. It is estimated that the average recurrence interval for large earthquakes ($M_s 8 \pm$) on this segment of the fault is on the order of 150 years. Central Los Angeles is approximately 35 miles southwest of the nearest point of the fault.

energy being away from the fault. In general, the larger the slipped fault area, the greater is the amount of strain energy released, the larger is the surface area affected by strong shaking, and the larger is the "felt area" of ground shaking.

For engineering purposes the magnitudes are approximate indices of the size of the earthquake; the local magnitude gives a measure of the strength of shaking and M_s indicates the area that might be affected by strong ground motion. In earthquake engineering practice, it is customarily assumed that two earthquakes having the same magnitude will have similar characteristics, including ground shaking, other things being equal; but it should be kept in mind that other things (tectonic setting, depth of rupture, rock type, fault mechanism, rate of activity, etc.) are seldom entirely equal.

The adequacy of seismological data for purposes of design depends upon having sufficient earthquakes in the historical record, with magnitudes and locations determined, so that large magnitude events are also included. For example, if the data include only earthquakes having $M_L < 5$ the probability distribution for large earthquakes would not be defined and it would be of questionable reliability to extrapolate to the probability of earthquakes of $M_s > 8$. Lacking sufficient data to define a probability distribution, it is customary in U.S. practice to assume a distribution for magnitudes that is consistent with the seismic history of California, even though this introduces a degree of uncertainty.

In the less seismic regions of the U.S., the seismological data are relatively few and are typically of poor quality. For example, in the eastern part of the country the available historical information on damaging earthquakes seldom includes the instrumentally determined local magnitude of the event but instead gives Modified Mercalli Intensity (MMI) numerals. The MMI index provides information of a lower quality than the magnitude, not only because it is based on personal observations of earthquake effects instead of instrumental records, but also because the actual interpretation is often unreliable. For example, a review of the effects of the August 12, 1929 Attica, New York, earthquake indicates a maximum MMI of VII instead of the VIII originally assigned to it (Ref. 3). The uncritical

29

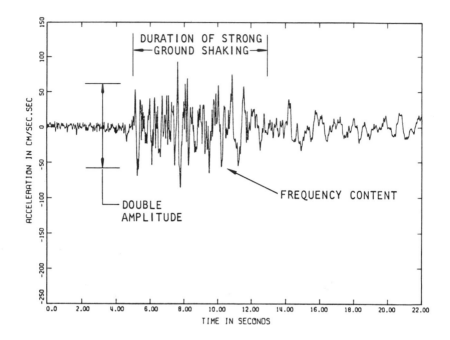

Figure 8. North-south ground acceleration recorded at California Institute of Technology during the $M_L6.4$ San Fernando earthquake (Feb. 9, 1971). The instrument was located 20 miles from the causative fault, and at this distance the duration of strong ground shaking was approximately 8 seconds, this being the same as the duration of the slipping process on the fault. The amplitude of acceleration was much greater at instruments closer to the fault.

use of MMI data introduces a degree of uncertainty which may lead to an overestimation of seismic hazard.

Geological Data

The seismic history of the United States, about one to three hundred years depending on location, is a relatively short time for assessing the frequency of earthquake occurrence. For reliable statistical studies to be made, the duration of the seismic history should be long compared to the average time between large earthquakes, a time which appears to range from as short as about one hundred years to several thousand years, depending on the degree of activity of the region. For example, major earthquakes away from continental margins, such as have occurred in central China and the central United States, appear to have the longest recurrence intervals.

The relatively short time information provided by seismological history can be supplemented by geological information about long-time tectonic processes that are measured in thousands or hundreds of thousands of years. For example, faults that can be identified as having experienced slip during the past hundreds, thousands, or tens of thousands of years provide information about the seismic hazard of a region, but it is a difficult scientific problem to quantify this information. The data available to the geologist consist primarily of evidences of fracture and movement in rocks and soils along the surface expressions of faults. In the case of major projects, trenches may be dug across suspected faults and the displacements of the soil and rock layers mapped in detail. For this purpose, it is particularly valuable to have easily identifiable strata whose continuity or offset can be demonstrated with confidence. To establish the date of movement on a fault or, if a stratum is continuous, to establish the minimum time since the last movement, it is necessary to find the age of the soil and rock formations. Carbon-14 dating methods applied to organic materials can give data on ages up to about 35,000 years, and other methods based on amino acids or the elements of the uranium decay series can be used to give estimates of much longer ages.

In the best cases, the geological evidence will be sufficient to

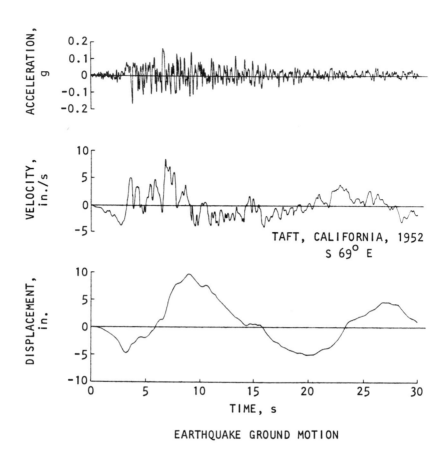

ACCELERATION, g

0.2
0.1
0
-0.1
-0.2

VELOCITY, in./s

10
5
0
-5

TAFT, CALIFORNIA, 1952
S 69° E

DISPLACEMENT, in.

10
5
0
-5
-10

0   5   10   15   20   25   30

TIME, s

EARTHQUAKE GROUND MOTION

Figure 9. Component S69E of horizontal ground shaking recorded at Taft, California during the M_s7.7 Tehachapi earthquake of July 21, 1952, at a distance of approximately 25 miles from the causative fault. This 0.18 g peak acceleration motion would be considered moderately strong shaking. The duration of strong shaking is greater for large magnitude earthquakes. The plots of ground velocity and ground displacement were obtained by integrating the acceleration record.

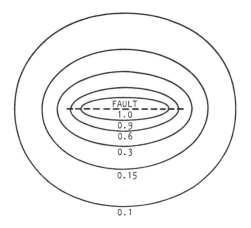

Figure 10. Idealized contour lines of equal intensity of ground shaking in the vicinity of an earthquake-generating fault that slipped over a length of 200 km. The severity of shaking attenuates with distance from the fault.

establish the length over which a fault has ruptured, the amount of cumulative fault displacement, and information about the period of time over which the movements have taken place. In addition, it is sometimes possible to make inferences concerning whether the fault has moved once, a few times, or many times during its active history. For faults that are active up to the present, geological data such as this can be used to help estimate the magnitudes and frequency of occurrence of earthquakes that may reasonably be expected in the future. It is equally useful if the geological data can be used to rule out the expectation of a specific fault generating an earthquake, which is an extremely important point for faults that may traverse or pass near the site of a critical facility and could pose a hazard both from shaking and fault displacement. If the undisturbed nature of the near surface geological materials can be established, this is conclusive evidence that the fault has not ruptured (and thereby generated an earthquake) since the formation of the oldest undisturbed material. Depending on the age of material and the critical nature of the facility under design, the lack of movement over an established number of years may eliminate the fault from further consideration in formulating the design criteria. For most ordinary construction, a fault that has not moved in Holo-

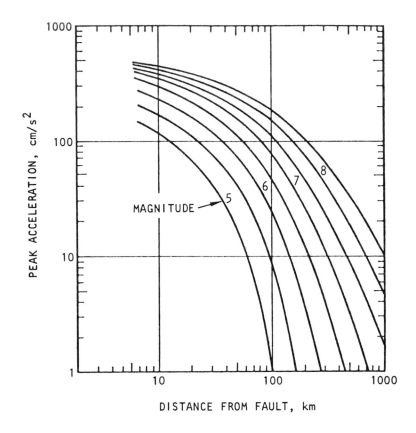

Figure 11. Idealized diagram showing how the intensity of ground shaking decreases with distance from the causative fault. For actual earthquakes the contour lines of equal intensity are not smooth but are irregular, reflecting the inhomogeneities in the earth's crust through which the seismic waves travel and also reflecting non-uniform movements along the fault. Close to the fault, the intensity of shaking can be affected by such things as depth of faulting, details of the rupturing process, etc.

cene times (the last 11,000 years) can be considered inactive, whereas for the design of nuclear plants, it has been ruled that a fault that has moved once in the last 35,000 years or more than once in the last 500,000 years must be considered as a possible source of future earthquakes.

Depending on the geological data and the judgment of the geologist, various procedures have been employed to interpret the seismic hazard posed by a given fault. The crudest approach is that which simply assigns a maximum size to the earthquake that the fault can generate. This earthquake is variously known as the Maximum Capable Earthquake, Maximum Credible Earthquake, Safe Shutdown Earthquake, Contingency Level Earthquake, etc. For example, a fault whose discernible length is approximately 40 miles might be assigned a Maximum Capable Earthquake (MCE) $M_s = 7$, or one with a discernible length of 15 miles might be assigned a MCE of $M_s = 6.5$. The MCE represents a "worst case" situation and by itself is not a very informative number, for it does not distinguish between a fault that will have events of the approximate size of the MCE once per 200 years and one for which the return period is once in 500,000 years, even though this information would be very important to engineers preparing seismic design criteria.

Seismological and Geological Information Required for Design

Project managers should require geological and seismological consultants to address the question of probability of occurrence. They should not accept a report that merely states "the recommended design earthquake is a Magnitude $M_s = 7.5$ at a distance of 20 km," not only because it gives no indication of frequency of occurrence but because the geoscientist has made a decision about engineering design which is outside his area of competence. The expertise of geological and seismological consultants is related to geologic and seismic hazards, and their reports should describe the possible earthquakes together with estimates of probability of occurrence, or the possible intensity of ground shaking together with its estimated probability of occurrence. The incorporation of the information into the design criteria should be the responsibility of persons who understand engineering design and performance of structures, and who can balance the hazard posed by earthquakes with that posed by other problems such as flooding and extreme winds.

A seismological report on a site will usually contain an estimate of the frequency of occurrence of earthquakes within a specified region. For a large, relatively seismic, region, such as the state of California, a rather good estimate can be made because of the large number of historical earthquakes. This is illustrated in the following table, which is derived from a smooth curve that approximates the seismicity of California.

TABLE 1. NUMBER OF EARTHQUAKES IN CALIFORNIA PER 100 YEARS HAVING MAGNITUDES ≥ M

M*	No.
4.0	8650
4.5	3340
5.0	796
5.5	351
6.0	122
6.5	45
7.0	18.5
7.5	5.5
8.0	1.5
8.5	0.1

*$M = M_s$ for 7.0 and greater; $M = M_L$ for smaller earthquakes

For smaller or less seismic regions within California, the historical record of earthquakes may contain so few events that estimates will be unreliable. Usually it is assumed that the distribution of earthquakes of various magnitudes within a portion is similar to the distribution for all California, and the California distribution is scaled to fit the historical record of the region. This might be described in the report by saying that N earthquakes of magnitude M, or greater, are expected in a 100 year

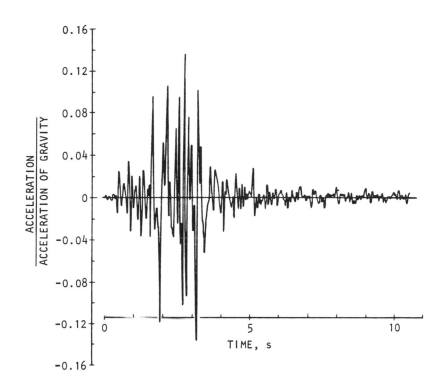

Figure 12. North-south component of ground acceleration recorded close to the epicenter of the Helena, Montana earthquake of October 31, 1935. The 3 seconds duration of strong shaking corresponds to $M_L 6 \pm$; shaking of this short duration could be damaging to weak and brittle structures, such as unreinforced masonry buildings.

37

period, and this would be sufficient for constructing the frequency distribution. For some regions of low seismicity it can be assumed that the probability of occurrence of very large earthquakes is negligibly small, but for other regions it may not be easy to decide whether or not the probability is negligible.

Strong motion accelerograms recorded in the past illustrate the kind of ground motions to be expected in the future, and the ground motion to be considered in the design can be described by three components of ground acceleration which are consistent with recorded accelerograms. The recommendations of an earthquake consultant should, preferably, present ground accelerations in the form of appropriate recorded accelerograms from particular earthquakes, or synthesized accelerograms that have appropriate intensity, duration, and frequency characteristics. The seismological consultant should also give the estimated probability of experiencing ground shaking more severe than this accelerogram. For example, it would be appropriate for him to give either the ground motion, which would be equalled or exceeded, with an average return period of 100 years, or the motion with an average return period of 200 years, so long as it is properly identified; but it would not be acceptable to give a ground motion without identifying its expected frequency of occurrence.

The estimates of frequency of occurrence are commonly given in one of two ways. The return period mentioned above is the average time between earthquake motions of a specified strength or greater; that is, 100-year earthquake motions would be expected 100 times in a 10,000 year period. The probability of an occurrence in any one year for an event with a return period R is $1/R$, and this can be used to calculate the probability of the occurrence in a longer period of time. For example, the probability of experiencing the shaking with a return period of 100 years in a given 100 year period is found by considering the probability of having at least one such shaking, and the probability of going through the entire 100 years without experiencing the event. These two probabilities cover all possibilities and must therefore add to unity, and since the probability of escaping the 100 year earthquake in one year is 0.99, and for two years is (0.99) (0.99), etc. We have the equation

$$P_{100} = 1 - (0.99)^{100} = 0.63$$

where P_{100} is the probability of occurrence of one or more ground motions with an average return period of 100 years, in a given 100-year period. With a 37% probability (that is, 0.99^{100} = .37) of not having an earthquake, $P_{100} = 0.63$, i.e., there is a 63% chance of experiencing the 100-year event in a given 100-year period (some 100 year periods may experience 2 or 3 such events). It may help to understand this result if a 10,000 mm string is considered, along which 100 knots are tied at random. The string is then cut into 100 mm lengths. Clearly, some segments will have no knots, many will have one, and some will have two or more knots in one segment. Sometimes, estimates of the occurrence of earthquakes or ground motions are put in this format, e.g., the shaking that has a 50% chance of being equalled or exceeded in 100 years. This is not the same as estimating the annual probability or the return period, but the two can be related through analyses of the type explained above.

Sometimes in reports detailing the earthquake hazard, the geotechnical or seismological consultants do not present accelerograms but instead give a less complete description of the ground motion. Properly, even this less complete description should include (a) the intensity of ground shaking, (b) the duration of strong ground shaking, (c) the frequency characteristics of the expected motion, and (d) the frequency of occurrence. The intensity of the ground shaking indicates to the engineer how severely his structures will vibrate, and the duration of strong ground shaking indicates the degree of damage to be expected if the structure is stressed beyond the elastic limit. The frequency characteristics of ground motion should be identified, for earthquakes in different parts of the world can have different frequency characteristics and therefore can have different effects on structures. Finally, the estimated frequency of occurrence of ground shaking is needed in determining the allowable level of response to the shaking.

Often the intensity of ground shaking is described by giving a value of peak acceleration, but by itself this is an ambiguous and oversimplified description, for two ground motions having the same peak acceleration can have appreciably different inten-

39

Figure 13. Collapsed freeway interchange bridge in the Sylmar region of Los Angeles. Five freeway bridges collapsed and 42 were damaged by the San Fernando earthquake; these structures were designed some years prior to the February 9, 1971 earthquake. Since then the designs of freeway bridges in California utilize dynamic analyses and other earthquake engineering research results.

sities so far as structural response is concerned. A much better method of describing the ground motion simply would be to compare it to a known accelerogram, such as recorded in Taft, California in 1952, or to a synthesized accelerogram. The description could thus be phrased as: 1.5 times as intense as Taft 1952, with a duration of strong shaking 1.2 times as long and with similar frequencies of motion. When the information is presented in this manner, the engineer can understand what the seismologist means and can use the information in constructing design spectra suitable for the project. More information can, of course, be given, but if any less information is given, the meaning will be ambiguous.

In some instances, the seismologist or geotechnical consultant may describe the ground motion by recommending a smooth "design spectrum," often tied to an estimate of the peak ground acceleration. This, however, is a mistake, for a "design spectrum" is not the same as a response spectrum of actual ground motion or a smoothed "average spectrum," and it is precisely this difference that involves engineering judgment. For example, removing the top 15% of the highest peak on an accelerogram would, in general, have very little effect on the computed response of structures. Therefore, when an engineer selects a smooth design spectrum based on an accelerogram or response spectrum, the zero-period spectral acceleration of the design spectrum may, with justification, be smaller than the peak ground acceleration. If the structure to be designed is highly ductile and ductile response to the motion under consideration is acceptable, the project manager may set the entire design spectrum at a lower level than the response spectrum of the design ground motion. The task of specifying the design spectrum depends on knowing how to correlate the spectrum with the properties of the structure to be designed.

Figure 14. Burning oil refinery in Niigata, Japan. The M7.5 (JMA scale) earthquake of June 16, 1964 damaged tanks and equipment, and this released oil that was ignited and burned uncontrolled for three days, consuming 350 homes. The fire continued to burn for two weeks. The Paloma Oil Refinery was similarly consumed by fire after being damaged by the July 21, 1952 Tehachapi, California earthquake.

Earthquake Response of Structures

To formulate suitable criteria for earthquake-resistant design, it is necessary to have an understanding of the way structures respond to strong shaking, including an appreciation of those dynamic properties of structures that affect the response to strong ground motion. It is also necessary to develop an understanding of the actual resistance, or capacity, of structures designed according to standard codes and procedures, as there are many factors which give typical structures a capacity much larger than indicated by such simple indices as, for example, the base shear coefficient implied by the factors in a building code.

One way to acquire some understanding of the way structures respond to very strong ground motions is to examine records of building motion obtained during strong ground shaking. The appendix of this monograph contains two such examples: The response of the Kajima International building recorded during the San Fernando earthquake of 1971, and the response measured in the heavily damaged Imperial County Services building during the Imperial Valley earthquake of 1979. The distinguishing feature of these examples is that they show what can be learned from accelerograms of earthquake response by straightforward examination, without the need for digitization and processing of the data and without the use of computing facilities beyond a hand calculator. Further understanding of the nature of earthquake response and the dynamic properties of structures can be gained by examination of the many earthquake damage reports and research studies that are available.

The Capacity of Structures

The data recorded in Fig. 15 provides additional insight into the capacity of typical structures to resist strong earthquake motions. These results, derived from the San Fernando earthquake of 1971, are for multistory reinforced concrete structures built since 1964. Figure 15 shows three sets of ordinates, all ex-

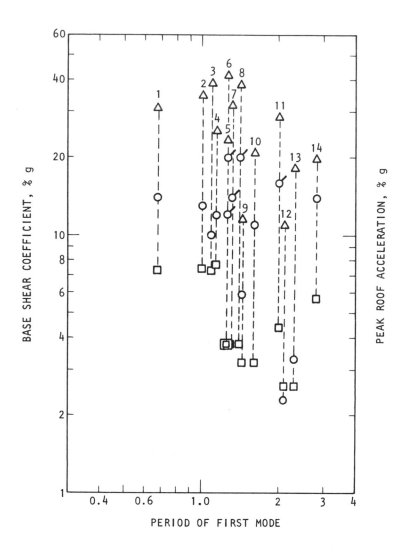

Figure 15. Plot of responses of 14 multistory concrete frame buildings during the San Fernando earthquake (Feb. 9, 1971). The triangles represent the peak acceleration recorded on the roof; the circles represent the peak base shear of the first mode as calculated from the recorded response of the building; the squares represent the design base shear as specified by the building code in Los Angeles. The ticked circles represent buildings that sustained some structural damage. The damage was not severe and none of the buildings were close to collapse. These were all relatively modern structures designed under the Los Angeles building code.

44

pressed in a percentage of gravity, plotted against the period observed for the fundamental mode of the building during the earthquake. The triangular data points, the top group, are the maximum accelerations measured on the roofs or top floors of the buildings. The circular data points represent the maximum base shears resulting from the fundamental modes of vibration of the structures. The base shears were determined from the maximum displacements, computed from the recorded accelerations, and from a knowledge of the distribution of mass in the buildings and the shapes of the fundamental modes. A ticked circle indicates that some structural damage was associated with this building and its base shear. It should be noted, however, that none of the structures represented in the figure were dangerously damaged, and it is believed that all could have resisted significantly stronger shaking without collapse. The square data points in the figure are the base shear values employed in the designs; these were determined by the designer in accordance with the applicable building code. One expected result that is clear from Fig. 15 is that the observed peak acceleration on the top level of the building is numerically greater than the base shear in the first mode, when both are expressed as percentages of gravity. This results from the geometry of the fundamental mode shape and also from the effects of higher modes on the peak acceleration. The most significant result in the figure, however, is that it indicates that structures of this type can, on the average, be expected to resist base shears that are two to three times larger than the code design values without major structural damage. The margin of safety against collapse of these structures was not tested by the San Fernando earthquake, but the data and the condition of the buildings suggest that responses equivalent to five or more times the design base shear could have been resisted without collapse, though severe damage would have resulted.

One of the main conclusions that can be drawn from study of the effects of earthquakes on structures is that the design base shear coefficient in the building code is not an accurate index of the true capacity of the structure, as built. Measurements of earthquake response as well as observation of the response of uninstrumented buildings show that typical buildings have

45

Figure 16. Olive View Hospital building after the San Fernando earthquake. The building was close to the center of energy release of the $M_L6.4$ quake. It was above the plane of the thrust fault and received very strong ground shaking having an estimated peak ground acceleration of $0.50\pm$ g. The building, which was essentially a heavy box on slender columns, was not designed to withstand such strong shaking.

Figure 17. Brittle failure of a tied corner column of the Olive View Hospital building.

Figure 18. Extreme deformation of a spirally reinforced interior column of the Olive View Hospital building. The ductile behavior of these columns prevented the collapse of the building.

47

greater earthquake resistance than is indicated by the base shear coefficient. Earthquake performances have also shown that the resistances of buildings are not necessarily proportional to the code requirements under which they were designed, for both architectural as well as engineering decisions influence the final result. This is illustrated by the contrasting performances of the Veterans Administration (VA) Hospital Building 41 during the 1971 San Fernando earthquake (Ref. 11) and the Imperial County Services building during the Imperial Valley earthquake of 1979 (Ref. 2). The study of VA Building 41 showed that the capacity of this shear wall structure at yield, with some load distribution, was in the range of 35–45% of its weight, whereas it was officially designed for 10% of its weight at working stress levels. The ground motion at the site had an estimated peak ground acceleration of 0.50 g or more, but the structure was not significantly damaged by the shaking; the capacity of the building was thought to be enhanced by good detailing in the design and by the favorable effects of nonlinear soil/structure interaction. On the other hand, the Imperial County Services building was heavily damaged with partial collapse of the columns at one end of the structure, even though it had been designed under a more modern code (1969 UBC) and was subjected to less intense ground shaking.

The concept of an actual resistive capacity beyond that indicated by the design coefficients has been implicit in seismic portions of building codes since their inception, but only recently have sufficient instrumental data become available to quantify this effect. The apparent paradox that the code value of acceleration for which a structure was designed is much smaller than the recorded peak acceleration of the ground motion that the structure successfully survived often causes confusion and has led to misunderstandings in the design of major projects. It is important to realize that the paradox can be explained without recourse to such terms as "effective peak acceleration" and "sustained peak acceleration," which are smaller than the peak acceleration itself. The explanation lies primarily in the fact that the allowable design stresses and strains in the building code are not directly indicative of the material and structural resistances under dynamic conditions. In addition,

Figure 19a. Two-story Psychiatric Building at Olive View Hospital after the San Fernando earthquake. The first-story columns collapsed during the earthquake.

Figure 19b. View of a disintegrated column of the Olive View Hospital. These light-weight concrete, tied columns were subjected to large strains during the earthquake vibrations, and the concrete shattered.

there are conservative features in codes and practices that add to the actual capacity of a structure. To clarify this situation it is necessary to establish the true relation between the dynamic capacity of engineered structures and the levels of the basic components of the design criteria. This represents one of the major challenges of earthquake engineering research.

If the observed ability of structures to resist earthquakes is not taken into account when formulating the design criteria, it is possible to end up with inconsistent results. For example, several reinforced concrete shear-wall buildings, including Building 41, survived the severe ground shaking at the VA Hospital site during the San Fernando earthquake without significant damage. However, these VA buildings probably could not satisfy the seismic design criteria set for the new, post-earthquake, Olive View Hospital building, at a site adjacent to the VA Hospital grounds.

Figure 20. Damage to the electrical switching gear at the Pacific Intertie during the San Fernando earthquake (Feb. 9, 1971). Strong shaking can damage equipment of all kinds if provisions have not been made for earthquake resistance.

From a combination of experiences with earthquake ground motions, measured responses of buildings, and detailed studies of individual structures, it is possible to estimate the capacity of structures of different broad types; such estimates are presented in Table 2. The table describes, for Southern California conditions, the expected performance of buildings of different types to the potentially damaging shaking that can occur in major earthquakes. The table provides a first approximation to the expected effects of strong ground motion.

To make more accurate calculations of the expected performance of structures is difficult because the processes of structural deterioration and collapse are complicated and cannot be related directly to some simple characteristic of the ground motion such as peak acceleration or duration. Rather, studies of collapse seem to indicate that the time taken to collapse for a given class of structures, even under a specified strength of intense shaking, is highly variable. The complexity is reduced, but is still considerable, if the response of a single structure to a given accelerogram is considered.

Assessing the Strength of Ground Motion

These considerations lead to the question of how to assess the strength of ground motion for the purposes of engineering design. As a rough rule-of-thumb and for discussions where precision is not required or justified, the historical practice of measurement by use of peak acceleration seems appropriate. For example, column two of Table 2, labeled 15–20%g, is a brief way of describing accelerograms with near average frequency content, duration and general form, with peaks in the range of 15–20% of gravity. When attempts are made to characterize ground motion more precisely, difficulties arise and no one-parameter characterization has proven satisfactory. The difficulties are fundamental: It is inherently impossible to describe a complex phenomenon by a single number, and a great deal of information is inevitably lost when this is attempted.

It is not surprising, then, that several measures of earthquake intensity have been put forward and that two and three parameter characterizations have also been attempted. The varying

51

TABLE 2. EXPECTED DEGREE OF DAMAGE IN SOUTHERN CALIFORNIA VS. SEVERITY OF SHAKING BASED ON SAN FERNANDO EARTHQUAKE

Class of Building	Severity of Ground Shaking			
	15–20% g	20–30% g	30–40% g	40–50% g
A–Above average modern building	None	Minor or none	Moderate	Severe
B–Average modern building	Minor or none	Moderate	Severe	Major
C–Below average modern building	Moderate	Severe	Major	Partial collapse
D–Old, pre-code building	Moderate to severe	Major	Partial collapse	Partial collapse

Minor Damage: can be repaired without appreciable interference with normal operations.

Moderate Damage: can be repaired with small interference with normal operations; perhaps equivalent to closing down for several days.

Severe Damage: significant damage to structural members; repairs will require closing for at least several weeks.

Major Damage: extensive damage to structural elements; repairs require closing down for several months.

Partial Collapse: repairs require closing down for an extended period, from five months to a year. For Class D structures the building may have to be abandoned.

results achieved by different measures are illustrated in Figs. 21 and 22, which show different accelerograms and how they rate according to different measures. The first column in Fig. 22 rates the accelerograms according to peak acceleration, wherein it is seen that the Pacoima record is far ahead of the others, followed by the Melendy ranch record. The rest of the accelerograms lie between 0.20 and 0.50 g. The second column shows the ranking when the spectrum intensity is used as a measure of strength. The spectrum intensity used for the figure is the area under the 20% damped response spectrum over a period range from 0.1 sec to 2.5 sec and is therefore an average measure of the response of linear structures in this range of periods. By this measure the Pacoima record is still the strongest, followed by Parkfield and the artificial earthquakes A-1 and A-2, which have moved up in comparison to their ranking by peak acceleration. The Melendy ranch record rates very low on this scale. The third column rates the accelerograms on the basis of the total energy in the records, that is, the integral of the square of the acceleration over its duration. In this case, the artificial earthquake records are the strongest, followed by Pacoima dam record, while the other records are about half as strong. The next two columns rate the accelerograms according to their ability to cause damage and collapse to a particular class of reinforced concrete structures. The damage acceleration, a_d, is the yield level required of the given class of structures to resist the accelerogram without serious damage. Similarly, a_c, represents the yield level of the class of structures needed to resist the acceleration without collapse, under the combined effects of strong shaking and gravity. The Pacoima and Parkfield accelerograms are the strongest by the damage rating, a_d, followed by the artificial earthquakes. Measured by the ability to cause collapse, a_c, the Pacoima accelerogram and the artificial earthquakes are the most severe, requiring yield levels of about 0.15 g for this class of structure to survive the shaking. The shorter accelerograms, Melendy ranch and Rocca, have high peak accelerations but can cause collapse only in structures with yield levels below about 0.005 g, far below realistic levels for modern structures.

Figure 22 illustrates the problems that arise in using simple

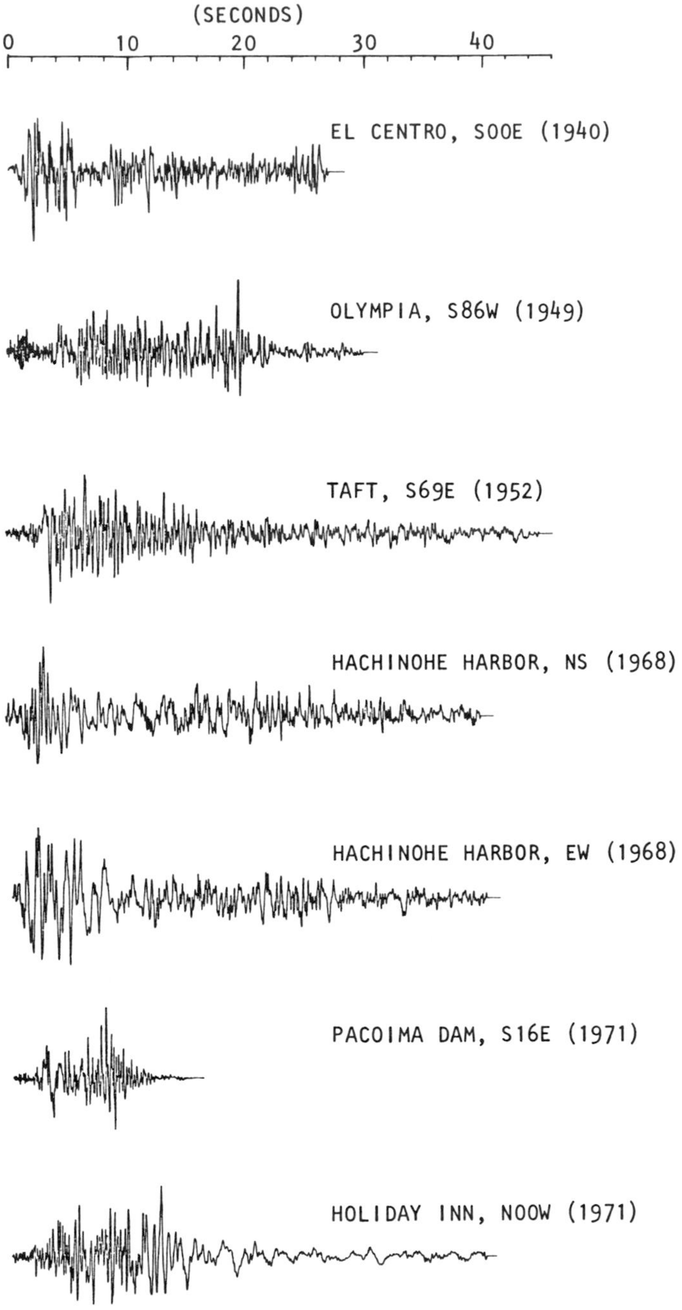

(SECONDS)

0   10   20   30   40

EL CENTRO, SOOE (1940)

OLYMPIA, S86W (1949)

TAFT, S69E (1952)

HACHINOHE HARBOR, NS (1968)

HACHINOHE HARBOR, EW (1968)

PACOIMA DAM, S16E (1971)

HOLIDAY INN, NOOW (1971)

(a)

54

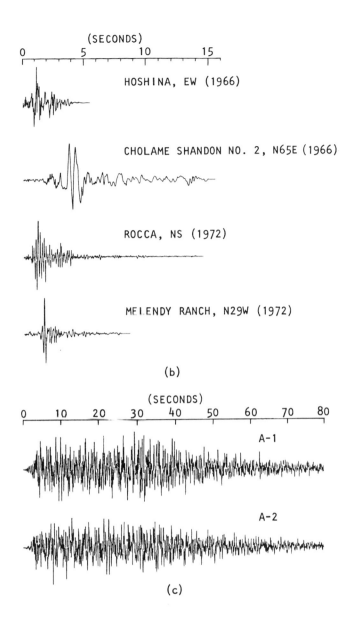

Figure 21. Accelerograms from different earthquakes. Group (a) shows accelerograms from $M_s = 6\frac{1}{2}$ to $7\frac{1}{2}$ earthquakes. Group (b) includes records obtained close to the fault in smaller earthquakes, plotted to a different time scale. The much longer records in group (c) are artificially generated accelerograms modeling the expected ground motion close to the fault in a great $(M_s = 8+)$ earthquake.

55

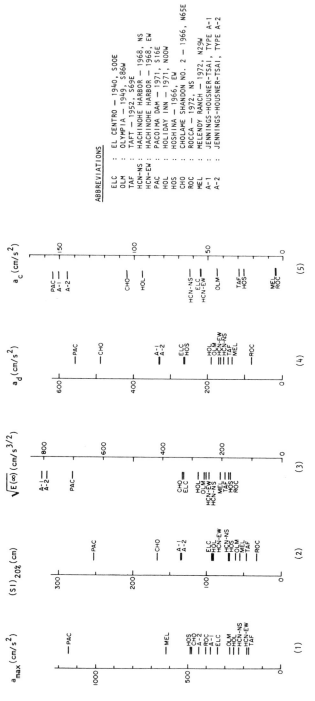

Figure 22. Ratings of accelerogram strength by different measures of the intensity of shaking. The accelerograms are identified in the list of abbreviations and are plotted in Figure 21. The measurements of intensity used are explained in the text. Note the change in rankings of the records according to the different measures. No single-parameter measure of strength of shaking has proved completely satisfactory; measuring strength by peak acceleration, though commonly used, is not entirely satisfactory.

measures of the strength of shaking, such as peak acceleration. The high peak acceleration for the Pacoima record gives a correct impression of its strength; it is a strong record by all common measures. On the other hand, peak acceleration gives a completely misleading impression of the destructive potential of accelerograms like Melendy ranch and Rocca, and seriously underestimates the strength of artificial records A–1 and A–2, which have most of their energies in lower frequencies than those that typically determine peak acceleration.

As a consequence of the problems discussed above, a design procedure that characterizes the ground motion by a single parameter of the wave form, for example, one which fixes the level of a predetermined spectral shape by equating the high frequency limit of the design spectrum to the expected peak ground acceleration, is often going to lead to unacceptably large inconsistencies in the design criteria. To continue the example, if the procedure cited is followed literally, the design criteria for an earthquake capable of generating the Melendy ranch record (M_L = 4.7 at a distance of 8.5 km) would be almost twice as great as required for a repeat of the El Centro 1940 shock (M_L = 6.5 at 20 km), and over three times that indicated for conditions like that which produced the Taft, 1952 record (M_L = 7.2 at 65 km). To do this would be absurd, considering the effects of these motions on engineered construction. In view of the large inconsistencies that can arise, it is surprising that standard practices of some regulatory agencies are based on this over-simplification.

Engineering Design Criteria

The framework for earthquake-resistant design criteria is provided by the seismological and geological data concerning earthquakes and their occurrence and by information about strong ground motion and structural response during earthquakes. The guiding principle in the selection of criteria is that they be consistent with the state of knowledge reflecting both what is known and what is unknown about earthquakes and structures. It is not suitable, for example, for design criteria to be sensitive to precise values of parameters that are beyond our present ability to predict accurately, such as the detailed frequency content of ground motion or the length of surface faulting. For quantities with this type of uncertainty, a simple, relatively insensitive specification that is not misleading about the state of knowledge, is more appropriate.

The Design Spectrum

The central item of most earthquake-resistant design criteria is the design spectrum; an example is shown in Fig. 23. Typically, a set of design spectra consists of smooth curves or a series of straight line segments, with one curve for each indicated value of damping. It is important to recognize the distinction between a design spectrum such as Fig. 23 and a response spectrum, Fig. 24. The jagged response spectrum is a plot of the maximum response of different oscillators to a given accelerogram and, hence, is a description of a particular ground motion. The smooth design spectrum, however, is a specification of the level of seismic design force, or displacement, as a function of natural period of vibration and damping level. The shapes of design spectra are determined, in some cases, from response spectra by smoothing out the peaks and valleys or by averaging several comparable response spectra. In other cases, the determination of the shape of the design spectra is more complicated because the same design spectra may have to reflect the potential shaking

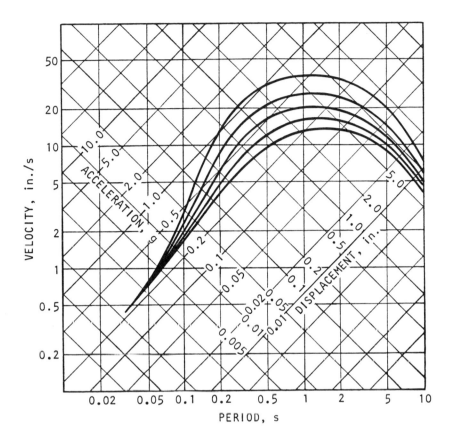

Figure 23. Example of smooth design spectrum based on Holiday Inn response spectrum, San Fernando earthquake of February 9, 1971 (0, .02, .05, .10, .20 of critical damping). Arriving at the right shape and amplitude for the smooth design spectrum requires good engineering judgment.

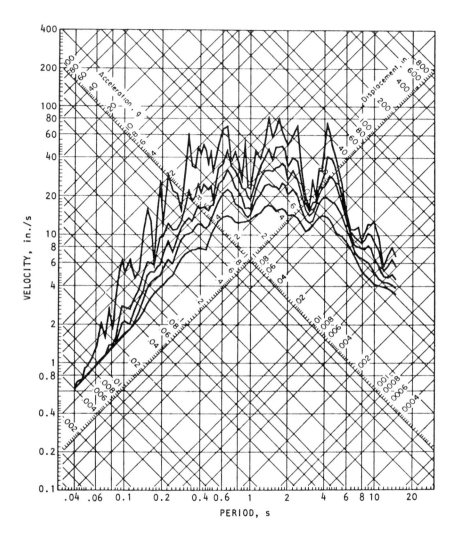

Figure 24. Response spectrum of north-south ground acceleration recorded at Holiday Inn, approximately five miles from the causative fault in the San Fernando earthquake of February 9, 1971 (0, .02, .05, .10, .20 of critical damping).

60

from different types of earthquakes. For instance, it would not be unusual for sites in California for the high frequency portion of the design spectra to be governed by the possibility of nearby earthquakes with local magnitudes near 6.5, while the low frequency portion of the design spectra would be controlled by the possibility of a great earthquake on the San Andreas Fault. In this case, the appropriate design spectrum is not simply determined by smoothing or averaging a set of response spectra. In any case, smoothing is performed in recognition of the fact that the detailed character of the response spectra of future earthquakes is unknown. A smooth, slowly varying curve is also more appropriate because of the difficulty in calculating exactly what the period of a structure will be during strong shaking and the fact that for very strong shaking, nonlinear response is expected.

An additional difference between design spectra and response spectra is that the design spectra have implications that are not shared by response spectra. Implicit in Fig. 23 is the condition that the level of force prescribed by a design spectrum is to be associated with a specified level of material resistance, for example, the allowable design stresses or strains. The resultant effect is, thus, a specification of the required earthquake resistance of the structure and its elements. If the material resistance is stated in terms of allowable stresses, the design spectrum is a specification of the strength of the structure; if the material resistance is expressed in terms of permissible ductile strains, the design spectrum becomes a specification of the capacity of the structure to deform, that is, the ductility it must have.

In trying to understand the relation between response spectra and design spectra, it is important also to realize the implications of some of the features of response spectra, particularly if ductile response is permitted in the event of very strong shaking. The response spectrum, by definition, is a plot of the maximum values of the responses of simple linear structures, which are reached only once during the response. (In theory, the maximum could be reached twice or more, but this remote possibility can be ignored). The other peaks of the response are less than the maximum, most of them much less. Typically, during a small earthquake, there will be only a few peaks within 25–30%

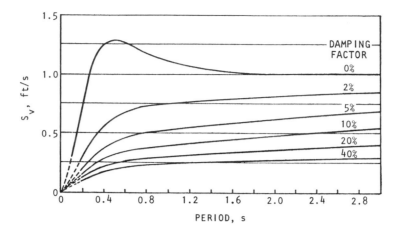

VELOCITY SPECTRUM CURVES

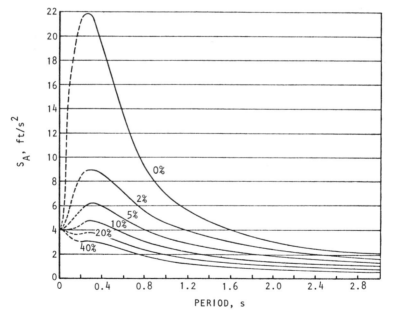

ACCELERATION SPECTRUM CURVES

Figure 25. Smooth design spectrum curves based on the average shapes of response spectra of several strong earthquakes. The curves are arbitrarily scaled to 0.125 g at zero period. These curves, developed by G. W. Housner in the 1950's, were the first design spectra used for the seismic design of structures (Ref. 5). The first response spectrum curves were developed at the California Institute of Technology in the early 1940's.

of the maximum, while in a larger, longer earthquake, the number of large peaks will, on the average, increase. It is important to the response of a ductile, degrading structure whether the maximum value is approached only three or four times, or whether values near the peak are approached ten or fifteen times. This is a factor to be considered in setting the level of the design criteria. This is not to say, however, that response spectra do not reflect the duration of shaking. They do, in the straightforward way that the longer the shaking, the bigger the maximum response is likely to be, other things being the same. This is particularly the case for small values of damping for which it takes a considerable time for the response to build up to a steady state, in a statistical sense. Even after the response has passed through the start-up phase, the maximum response of a linear structure still increases somewhat with the duration of strong shaking, since in the longer duration there is a bigger chance for an unusually large response to occur. In assessments of the effect of duration of shaking, the best way to measure the duration is in terms of multiples of the fundamental vibrational period of the structure.

From the preceding discussion, it should be clear that the suitability of design criteria cannot be judged solely by the level of the design spectra; there are four major factors which combine to determine the capacity of structures to resist earthquakes: (1) the level of the design spectra; (2) the designated spectral damping; (3) the permissible stresses and strains; and (4) the method of determining the natural periods of vibration of the structure. It is customarily considered that the level of the design spectra is the most important, but because of their combined effects the other three factors together can be just as important. For example, Fig. 26, which is a replotting of the design spectra in Fig. 23, shows the effect that damping has on the design acceleration. The effect is very strong for damping less than 0.1 of critical and for periods less than 2 seconds. Table 3 shows that the same spectral acceleration (0.54 g) is obtained when the design spectrum level at zero period is .21 g, or when it is 25% larger or 25% smaller, if suitable adjustments are made in the other parameters.

63

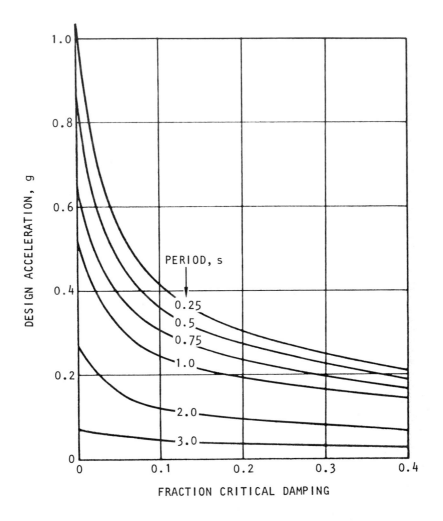

Figure 26. The design spectrum of Figure 23 replotted to illustrate the effect of damping on spectrum values.

TABLE 3. EFFECT OF DAMPING AND PERIOD ON DESIGN CRITERIA

	A	B	C
Design spectrum level at zero period (g)	.16	.21	.26
Damping	.03	.04	.05
Natural period (sec)	.35	.4	.5
Allowable stress or strain (relative value)	.9	1.0	1.2
Spectral acceleration (g)	.54	.54	.54

This simple illustration is intended to show that the design criteria can be incomplete unless all four of the factors involved are specified.

In setting the design criteria, one should take into account the acceptable degree of damage and the likelihood of its occurrence. It is also necessary to consider the actual capacity of the structure that results from the use of the design spectra and the specified capacities, both strength and toughness, of the materials of construction. This is obviously a problem requiring both engineering knowledge and judgment and, because of the complexities and uncertainties, considerable reliance must be placed on knowledge of how engineered structures of similar types have performed during past earthquakes. For example, the San Fernando earthquake provided abundant evidence that the level of design criteria, together with the allowable material resistances and the quality control and inspection specified in California's Field Act, ensure the successful performance of typical one- and two-story school buildings during very strong shaking (Ref. 6). The schools performed successfully even though the nominal code levels of earthquake forces were much lower than the actual base shears or the peak accelerations of the ground shaking.

Modifications in the Shape of the Design Spectrum

In order to specify consistent levels of structural capacity for structures having different natural periods, the shape of the

Figure 27. Holiday Inn building at 8244 Orion Boulevard in Van Nuys after the San Fernando earthquake (Feb. 9, 1971). The building was located approximately 5 miles south of the nearest portion of the surface trace of the fault. The peak ground acceleration was 0.28 g and, although no significant damage is visible on the exterior, some of the reinforced concrete beams and columns sustained cracking, which was later repaired with epoxy glue. The interior of this hotel building suffered extensive nonstructural damage. The motions recorded during the earthquake on the ground floor and the roof are shown in Figures 28 and 29.

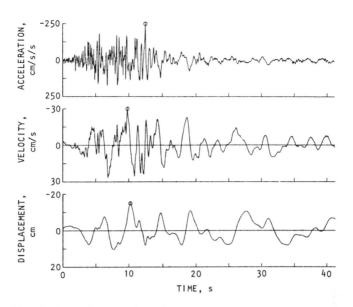

Figure 28. North-south ground motion at Holiday Inn during the San Fernando earthquake. The accelerograph was approximately five miles from the
closest portion of the causative fault of this $M_L6.4$ earthquake.

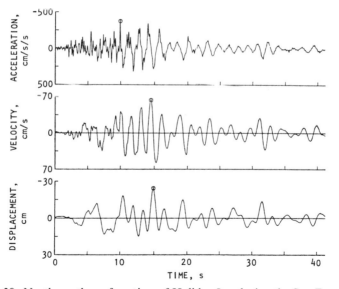

Figure 29. North-south roof motion of Holiday Inn during the San Fernando
earthquake. This building is a 7-story reinforced concrete frame building.
These recorded building motions enabled an analysis to be made of the stresses
and strains in the structure during the earthquake.

design spectra should reflect the relative intensities of ground motion expected at different frequencies. As noted above, the different frequency ranges of the design spectra may be controlled by different sizes and locations of earthquakes. Several earthquake engineers have examined this problem and have developed spectral shapes that are intended for general applications. Typically, only the overall amplitude, not the shape, is changed for a particular site. These design spectra are often well suited for inclusion in the design criteria, or are used as a starting point for the selection of more site-specific design spectra. The question then arises: What modifications in the shape of the design spectra should be made to accommodate the particular situation at the site under consideration? The most important point to remember is that it is not justified to go to great lengths in tailoring the shape of the design spectra to fit hypothetical earthquake hazards, for the present state of knowledge does not warrant this. It is quite in order to consider the possible effects of different kinds of earthquakes and structural performance, but when these considerations are translated into changes in the design spectra it is recommended that such modifications be limited in nearly all cases to simple and relatively minor alterations to spectra of standard shape.

The problem most often arises concerning the adjustment of design spectra to accommodate possible influences of local geology and soil conditions. Unfortunately, there is a lack of good data bearing directly on this problem, and such data accumulate slowly because of the cost of necessary instrumentation and because of the infrequent occurrence of strong earthquakes. To throw light on the possible effects of local soil conditions, special computations are often made which involve estimating the ground motion at depth (bedrock or firm soil), and then propagating this motion to the surface through linear or nonlinear models of the overlying soils. The seismic waves are assumed to be planar, horizontal shear waves that propagate vertically. Such analyses are often made for major projects sited on relatively soft soil. They can give useful insight if the actual geological and seismological conditions do not differ greatly from the conditions postulated by the computational procedures, as was the case, for example, of the well-known recorded be-

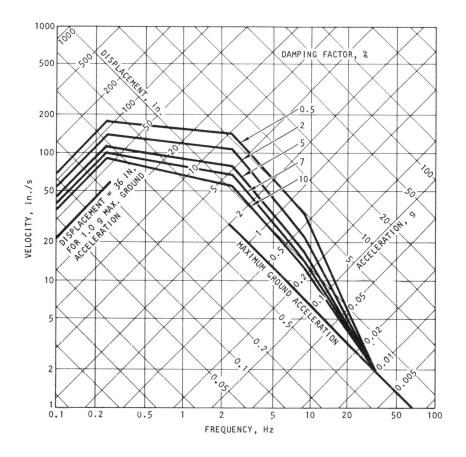

Figure 30. Design spectrum curves used for the design of nuclear power plants. Plotting design spectrum curves with straight line segments was first done by N. M. Newmark in the late 1960's. The design spectrum reproduced here (horizontal component) is from NRC Regulatory Guide 1.60 and was developed by Newmark, Blume and Kapur in the early 1970's (Ref. 16).

havior of the soft soil in Mexico City. However, it is very difficult to assess the differences between the assumed and the actual conditions, and in practice this approach has sometimes been misused. The difficulties that result in trying to assess potential site effects could be reduced by making careful comparisons of predicted results with existing accelerograms that were recorded under similar geological and seismological conditions. Such relevant accelerograms, if available, should be used as a primary guide in the adjustment of the shape of the design spectrum, and the results of analytical and computational studies should be used as secondary guides.

Selection of Damping Values for Design

The specification of the design criteria requires selection of damping values whether the response is to be constrained to the elastic region or whether ductile response is allowed. Efforts to calculate damping are still in the very early stages and values for design are determined from experience; the primary source of observed information is the measured response of structures during earthquakes and full-scale vibration tests. The observations show the damping to increase with the amplitude of response, with typical buildings showing values near 1 to 2% during vibration tests that are at relatively low levels of response. The damping values increase as the motion gets larger and the values deduced from strong earthquake responses lie mostly in the 5 to 10% range (see App. A). These are values of equivalent viscous damping, equivalent in the sense that they are the values of damping that give a calculated response in closest agreement with that recorded during strong shaking. The damping in buildings and other structures is not viscous and is believed to be a result of a combination of effects, including cracking, rubbing of nonstructural elements, and small amounts of yielding and cracking in structural members. The use of an equivalent damping factor in such a straightforward way is a practical design approach if the response of the structure does not substantially exceed the elastic range.

In selecting damping factors for design criteria that allow significant amounts of yielding under very strong shaking, the

70

role of equivalent damping becomes less clear. Records of strong earthquake response are sometimes matched best by linear structures with dampings of 15% or more, but the matching also requires a change in period of a factor of three or more, which implies a major loss of structural stiffness. Furthermore, the structures that exhibit such large dampings are observed to be responding in the range where significant yielding and structural damage are occurring. In designing for this range of response, it is not appropriate to reduce the design spectra by taking benefit of both ductile response and high damping. What seems to be the best approach is to select a value of damping that is representative of non-damaging response, and that can be associated reasonably with mechanisms in the structure that are still operating during the larger, ductile response.

If it is necessary to go beyond these simple approaches, the recommended procedure is to examine research studies of the response of yielding structures or to integrate the equations of motion of the structure subjected to earthquake motions. This level of effort seems to be required because of the inherent limitations of the concept of equivalent viscous damping, which becomes a gross oversimplification as the response becomes more and more nonlinear. Energy loss during structural vibrations is still a research problem.

Specification of Ductility

Extremely strong ground shaking at a given site is very rare, and most structures complete their life of useful service without experiencing shaking of the level of ground motion specified, for example, by the Maximum Capable Earthquake. Under these circumstances, it is unrealistically conservative and expensive, in most cases, to design the structure to respond to such shaking wholly within the elastic range of the materials involved. Instead, the intended response is ductile: structural members are allowed to yield and make significant excursions beyond the elastic range, but the structural damage is to be controlled and the structural integrity preserved, so the structure does not pose an undue hazard to life and limb. To design for limited damage

71

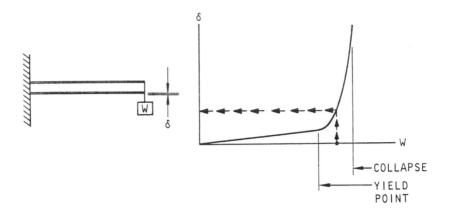

Figure 31. Force controlled displacement of a steel beam by weight W. As the weight W is increased, the displacement increases until yield point stress is reached. If W is given an additional increment (about 15%), a plastic hinge forms giving large displacements. For this kind of a system, yield point stress is close to collapse, as discussed in Figures 32 and 33.

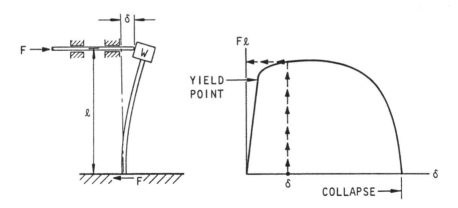

Figure 32. Displacement controlled deflection of a simple oscillator with a steel column. As the displacement is increased, the base moment F1 increases until the yield point is reached. As the displacement increases still more, the base moment increases only a small amount. The displacement can be increased 10 to 20 times the yield point displacement before the system collapses under the action of weight W. During an earthquake the oscillator is excited into vibrations by the ground motion and it behaves essentially as a displacement controlled system and can survive displacements much beyond the yield point. This explains why ductile structures can survive ground shaking that produces displacements much greater than the yield point displacement.

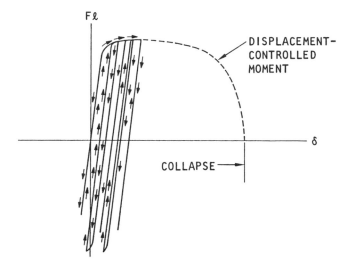

Figure 33. Illustrative example of how a simple oscillator will behave during strong ground shaking that produces ductile strains. Although plastic straining may take place in both directions, there is a tendency for weight W to bias the motion toward one direction and this eventually leads to collapse, even if there is ample ductility. Without sufficient ductility, failure and collapse can result sooner.

is clearly a more difficult engineering problem than designing for elastic response.

Ductility is normally measured by the ratio of the overall displacement of the structure to that at the elastic limit. This is not a precise definition, as the deformation pattern of a complex structure may be different in the two cases, but it can be made exact for one-degree-of-freedom structures, and can be applied approximately to structures with more degrees of freedom if the deformation pattern for the nonlinear response is specified. The additional concept of member or local ductility is sometimes used. The need for this concept arises, for example, because a girder in a building might have to form a plastic hinge with rotation sixteen times the elastic rotation in order for the overall building frame to deflect four times its maximum elastic deflection.

The amount of ductility permitted in the design should be

73

determined by the need to preserve the basic safety of occupants or other affected personnel and by the costs of the damage implied by the ductile response. It is important in assessing such costs to consider all the relevant factors, including structural and nonstructural repairs, loss of production or operation, employee losses, as well as intangibles such as possible loss of prestige or goodwill. Once safety is assured, the cost of the expected damage to the facility or structure after the earthquake determines the allowable ductility, and this decision should properly be made by the owner. In practice, however, the owners are often not prepared, or disposed, to make this decision and it is made, in default, by the project engineer. A better procedure would be for the engineer to meet with the owner and present him with a range of allowed ductilities and their resulting costs and benefits. It also helps to know, of course, what is the standard practice for structures of this general type, as this helps the owner decide what to do in his case.

The Use of Accelerograms and Artificial Earthquake Records

Dynamic analysis employing design spectra is usually a sufficient procedure for the earthquake-resistant design of structures and facilities. The design spectra specify the maximum responses of each mode of a complex structure and approximate methods are available to combine the modal responses to get total values of quantities of interest. There are circumstances, however, where this procedure is not appropriate or sufficiently accurate to supply the information required for design. What then can be done is to solve the equations of motion of a mathematical model of the structure on a computer, using, as excitations, recorded accelerograms or artificial accelerograms constructed for this purpose. The three principal reasons for undertaking this more involved and expensive analysis are to determine input motions for important pieces of equipment in the structure, to develop examples of the way modal responses are actually combining rather than relying on approximate methods of combination, and to determine the expected response of nonlinear systems to earthquake motions.

74

When designing important equipment to resist earthquakes, it is necessary to take into account the fact that the equipment will receive different shaking, for example, if it is on the ground floor of a building or if it is on the roof. Approximate ways to handle this problem have been developed, but it is also possible to integrate the equations of motion of the structure, recover the acceleration at the point where the equipment is to be mounted, and use this motion to generate "floor response spectra" that can guide the development of design spectra for the equipment in a way similar to the use of response spectra of ground motion in constructing design spectra. This procedure is simple in concept and has the advantage that it does not require information about the equipment to construct the floor-response spectra, so a change of equipment does not require another calculation. The procedure breaks down, however, if the fixed-base response of the equipment is very near one of the natural frequencies of the main structure. In this case the equipment is excited into vibrations by the motion of the floor, and the duration of the floor motion has an important influence on the equipment response. In this, the so-called "tuned" case, the simple procedure mentioned can greatly overestimate the response of the equipment and it is necessary either to use the results of analytical studies (Ref. 12) or to integrate the equations of motion of the structure with the equipment included as well as the structure.

Aside from the question of the response of equipment, the main reason to integrate the equations of motion of a linear structure excited by ground motion, rather than use the simpler analysis based on the design spectra, is to see how the modes of the system are actually combining. The spectral approach gives the desired maximum value of each modal response; it is the method of combination of the modes that is approximate. The need to examine the way modes combine can arise in cases where the structure has a number of modes with nearly equal frequencies. Such modes will respond to the earthquake in a similar, correlated manner, so combining modal responses by common procedures, such as by the square root of the sum of the squares, may indicate a response of the structure that is too low. Closely-spaced natural frequencies can arise in dams,

75

suspension bridges and other large systems. Two or three closely-spaced modes can also arise in the case of buildings, offshore drilling platforms and liquid storage tanks. For example, the natural frequencies of the two translational fundamental modes can be nearly equal. The near-field ground motion in some major earthquakes contains large pulses that can make two modes of about the same frequency respond in a highly correlated manner. This problem can be addressed by use of accelerograms as noted, but it can be also treated by use of design spectra if the modal responses believed to be correlated are combined conservatively by adding their absolute values.

In some projects it may be feasible to make numerical investigations of how the structure or facility responds when driven into the nonlinear, yielding range of the materials. Such studies comprise an important part of earthquake engineering research, but the cost of the analysis and the uncertainties in the mathematical modeling have, to date, limited their use in practice. A structure responding nonlinearly to earthquake motion no longer possesses normal modes, and other features of the linear range of response, such as superposition, are lost as well. Once the linear range of response has been appreciably exceeded, it is no longer valid to analyze the structure by means of modal analyses, and other methods must be used. In some cases, the response may be studied by means of equivalent linearization in which the nonlinear structure is matched as well as can be by an associated linear structure, which can be analyzed more readily. The most general method of approach, however, is to integrate the equations of motion of the nonlinear structure on the digital computer, using representative earthquake motions as excitation. The procedure is straightforward in concept, but can be very costly and time-consuming to perform.

In making calculations of the type discussed above, the desired excitations would be a small sample of accelerograms that are representative of the shaking expected in the design earthquake and embodied in the design spectra. For example, in designing tall buildings in Southern California, one might wish to use as excitation several accelerograms obtained from $M_s = 8 +$ earthquakes at distances of about 30 miles. Such records are not yet available; in particular there is a scarcity of near-field

Figure 34. Extensive wall cracking of the Indian Hills Medical Center building in San Fernando Valley. This structure resisted earthquake forces by means of four vertical wall-type cantilever beams in each direction. The beams were strained much beyond the point of initial shear-cracking during the 1971 San Fernando earthquake without losing resistive capacity. The photograph shows one of the cantilevers during treatment to repair the cracks by means of epoxy, which makes the cracks visible. The ground motion at this location is estimated to have had a peak acceleration of 0.40 g, which could be expected to deform the cantilevers far beyond initial cracking. In view of this, it can be said that the cantilevers behaved very well. (It was found that the epoxy treatment did not restore the cantilevers to the pre-earthquake strength, so new vertical cantilevers were poured adjacent to the cracked ones.)

accelerograms in major earthquakes, and at this time none exist for earthquakes of the magnitude expected to recur on the San Andreas fault. To overcome this deficiency, artificial accelerograms have been constructed on the computer to represent a variety of conditions. The accelerograms are generated using results from the theory of random processes and typically represent a simple statistical characterization of strong ground motion with a frequency content adjusted to fit observations. The relative amplitudes of the artificial accelerograms as a function of time, and their durations can be adjusted to be similar to real motions, and the overall amplitude of the artificial record can be scaled to represent the desired condition for a particular site. In the distant future, there may exist enough recorded accelerograms to eliminate the need for artificial earthquakes in design studies, but in the meantime they serve a useful purpose. Also, they are simpler to use in statistical analyses than real accelerograms and are therefore useful in research studies where it is necessary to distinguish differences in response arising from structural variations from those caused by different excitations.

Most engineering research on generating artificial ground motions has used statistical models of the shaking and empirical methods of shaping and scaling the artificial motions. In recent years, seismological research on strong ground motion has advanced rapidly and the scientists have approached the problem from a different viewpoint. In modeling strong ground motion of an observed earthquake, seismologists use distant seismographic records to estimate overall features of the event, such as the extent, depth and orientation of the faulting. They then postulate a source mechanism and allow it to spread over the fault with various amplitudes consistent with observations of surface faulting. By superposing motions from all the small ruptures that make up the earthquake, the ground motion at any given point can be calculated and compared with data. The process is repeated on a trial and error basis until the data has a "best fit," then the motion at other sites can be estimated. When applied to the design of major facilities, this process can provide another way of looking at the motions that might occur, particularly those of larger periods (greater than 2–3 seconds) where the procedure seems to give the best results. The method is not yet suitable for calculating accelerograms of hypothetical future earthquakes.

The Role of Statistical and Probabilistic Analyses

In earthquake engineering there are many situations where essential factors cannot be defined precisely because of a lack of information. For example, the physical properties of the particular batch of concrete and steel are not known precisely to the engineer when he makes the design; and the quality of workmanship in construction is not known. These could be found by means of additional quality control, testing and inspection but the cost would be prohibitive, so the uncertainties are accepted. In this case, it is considered to be cost-efficient to accept and to deal with uncertainties rather than to try to eliminate them. In the case of earthquake ground motions, it is uncertain where and when earthquakes will occur and how large they will be, and it is not known what ground motions they will produce. Again, in principle, these uncertainties could be reduced to small levels, for the problem is solvable if the state of stress in the earth's crust were precisely known, and if the failure strength of the rock were known, and if all the relevant physical properties of the earth's crust through which the seismic waves travel were also known; and if sufficient time and money were available for computing. The difficulty and cost involved make it unlikely that this type of problem will ever be solved and it is necessary, therefore, to accept a lack of knowledge and to deal with it as well as possible. Statistical and probabilistic analyses are tools for dealing with scientific ignorance. Though they cannot generate factual information not already included in the basic data, such analyses provide different and occasionally subtle ways of making assumptions about the basic data which can provide useful guidance for making decisions. Because of their subtle nature, however, assumptions that are injudicious can be misleading.

When formulating design criteria it is necessary to specify the ground motion that the structures must be designed to resist. As the characteristics of future ground motion are not known, it is necessary to utilize other information that bears on the problem, for example, statistical information on the past occurrence of earthquakes of various magnitudes. If it were known where earthquakes will occur in the future and how large they will be, estimation could be made of the ground shaking at the site. This knowledge, however, is not available; what is known is where earthquakes have occurred in the past. The seismic history of a region of area A conveys information about the future only in the sense that the seismicity S of the past N years provides a data sample that is assumed to be more or less like the seismic events that will occur during the coming N years. The degree of similarity depends on the product SNA, there being little similarity for small values and greater similarity for large values. For a 200 year period in California, SNA = S x (150,000 sq mi) x (200 yr) = S x 3 x 10^7, and this promises a relatively high degree of similarity; but for N = 20 years or for A = 15,000 sq mi, only a low similarity can be expected, i.e., SNA = S x 3 x 10^6. The foregoing figures indicate that for regions having significantly lower seismicity than California, or for smaller areas, future seismicity probably will not bear close similarity to historical seismicity for the same period of years, and in order to draw conclusions it is necessary to assume a shape for the long-time frequency distribution of earthquakes in the area. This assumption permits statements to be made about probability of occurrence. A useful way of making probabilistic statements is to put them in a comparative form, for example, comparison with the seismicity of the State of California, which is fairly well known.

Because the store of records of strong ground motion is deficient in close-in, major earthquakes that usually control the design of a facility, regression analyses have been used to estimate the parameters of the expected ground motion. In these methods what is done, for example, is to select a sample of accelerograms recorded under the same general type of tectonic and site conditions as the design earthquake, but over a range of distances and magnitudes. Then, some single parameter of the ground motion such as peak ground acceleration, ground velocity or some spectral ordinate is plotted as a function of distance and magnitude, and mean and standard deviation curves are found by regression analysis. This usually takes the form of finding best-fit constants in an empirical formula giving the parameter of motion as a function of distance and magnitude. This kind of calculation is a good example of a case where the statistical assumptions involve subtleties. Beginning with any reasonable empirical formula, i.e., one where the ground motion parameter can decrease with distance and increase with magnitude, the scatter in the recorded ground motion is sufficiently large that the formula can be made to fit the data for those ranges of distance and magnitude where most of the data lie. Large differences are obtained when the relations are extrapolated back to the near field where few data are available. In this use the form of the original empirical formula becomes much more significant, as does the character and number of records in the sample and the nature of the regression analysis (e.g., logarithmic or linear). In addition, the implicit assumption in the regression calculations for the constants in the formula is that all the data are equally relevant. Also, unless a range of spectral ordinates is used, rather than one parameter like peak acceleration, the assumption is made that the ground motion can be characterized by a single parameter. It is obvious that these assumptions are questionable and are clearly different from an approach that constructs a design spectrum based on examination of response spectra from accelerograms recorded under conditions of magnitude and distance similar to that of the event considered in the design.

Regression analyses work best where they are used to describe observed variations in data. When there is ample data, they can be used to detect differences that are not obvious by other means. In this sense they have become a common tool, for example, in medical research where they can assess different rates of cure for different drugs. As a tool for extrapolation they are clearly less reliable, and their use in earthquake engineering to characterize ground motion for design should be supported by other, more direct methods.

Conservatism and Review Committees

Earthquake-resistant design, like other engineering design, has the objective of achieving a functional and economical design in the face of imprecise knowledge of the forces that will act upon the structure. Because of the imprecision in knowing the loads and the need for a safe design, most structures have substantial margins-of-safety for the loads they actually receive in their lifetimes. They are overdesigned in the sense that lack of knowledge about earthquake forces and other loads leads to a resistive capacity that will not be fully utilized. This margin-of-safety, or conservatism, is a necessary way of treating the uncertainties that are inevitable in the design of a major project. It is particularly appropriate to have substantial margins-of-safety in critical facilities such as nuclear reactors and major dams, where failure could pose a major hazard to public safety.

For earthquake-resistant design, the interplay between the conservatism in the design and the uncertainties in the earthquake response can be described in statistical terms in which uncertainties about the intensity of earthquake shaking and the degree of earthquake resistance are stated in terms of probabilities of occurrence and probabilities of amplitudes of response. Although no structure will ever achieve a zero probability of failure, the probability of failure can be reduced by the provision of extra resistance. The question then arises as to how small a probability of failure should be in order to be deemed an acceptable risk. No satisfactory method for making this socio-technological decision has yet evolved, so the determination of the appropriate level of conservatism by probabalistic means is open to question.

In construction governed by building codes and in certain projects, conservatism in the design is implicit in the sense that the design criteria in codes are established by subjectively taking into account the nature and levels of forces, the types and quality of construction, the properties of materials, and the experience of structures during earthquakes. A determination of the margin-of-safety in each particular portion of the specifications is not attempted and the overall margin-of-safety of typical buildings is not precisely known. In fact, it is considered by experienced engineers to be quite variable.

In the case of special projects, the problem should be approached explicitly; each feature of the problem should be examined separately and a decision made concerning its appropriate level. This approach has the advantage that each important aspect of the project is subjected to careful study by knowledgeable professionals and the chance of overlooking some important point is minimized. However, a difficulty is inherent in this approach, for unless someone keeps an overall check on the procedure, there is a danger of compounding the margin-of-safety in the sequence of decisions that leads to the earthquake-resistant design criteria. For example, if the geologist is conservative by a factor of 1.5 on the capability of faults in the area of the site, the seismologist 1.5 times conservative on the strength of expected shaking, and the design engineer 1.5 times conservative on the allowable material responses, the final conservatism compounds to 340%. Figure 35 shows the sensitivity of the overall factor of safety to the number of sequential steps and the individual factors of safety. Without some overall assessment of the conservatism, design criteria can become excessively conservative.

Compounding of conservatisms can also occur when the design criteria are reviewed by regulatory agencies or political bodies. In the best of circumstances, the review panels are composed of knowledgeable people with access to consultants who are expert in various specialized aspects of the earthquake problem. It is not usual, however, for any single panel member to have an overall view comparable to that of the project engineer, so the review tends to focus on those features of the problem that lie within the experience of the panel members and their consultants, and extra conservatism is often introduced at these points without consideration of the conservatism in the other parts of the design criteria.

The situation is even more difficult if knowledgeable engineers and scientists are not taking leading roles in the regulatory process; then psychological factors become more important. For example, one obvious way for a reviewing agency to make it appear that a good job is being done is to require increased design criteria. To a degree, the reviewers have their reputations at stake and in many cases the hearings of the reviewing panel are court-like in manner and open to the public. Because the reviewers are not directly answerable for the cost of the earthquake protection, these features of the review procedure tend to emphasize problems over the means and costs of providing solutions to problems. Hence, the outcome of the regulatory process tends to be a very stringent set of earthquake-resistant design criteria; the end result tends to approach an upper bound of the judgments of all the individual parties involved, rather than a compromise value. Experienced engineers term this the "ratchet effect."

Another factor that should be considered when dealing with regulatory agencies is the requirement to solve a problem in several ways. This arises from another fact of human nature: a regulatory body can demonstrate that it is doing its job by

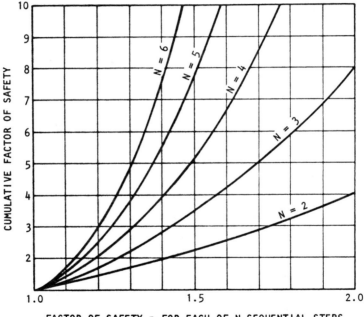

FACTOR OF SAFETY n FOR EACH OF N SEQUENTIAL STEPS

Figure 35. Chart showing the effect of superposing factors of safety. If the same factor of safety n is imposed in N sequential steps, the cumulative factor of safety becomes large. For example, if a factor of safety of 1.5 is put on the estimated magnitude, the same factor is put on the estimated ground acceleration, and then on the computed stresses, and on the allowable stresses: n = 1.5, N = 4 and the cumulative factor of safety ≅ 5. When setting the design criteria, it is important that any superposition be identified so that the cumulative factor of safety has the desired value.

requesting information not included in the material under review. Thus, if one method has been used to determine earthquake-resistant design criteria, there is a tendency for the reviewing panel to ask how the result compares to that obtained by another approach. This, of course, is often a very legitimate question. Therefore, the project engineer should consider several approaches to major problems in setting design criteria and be prepared to discuss them.

It is easier to comment critically on the reviews of seismic design criteria by regulatory bodies than it is to suggest alternative procedures. One helpful step would be to involve more knowledgeable engineers in the reviewing process. The engineering viewpoint is always well represented on the side of those applying to regulatory bodies, but it is often underrepresented on the reviewing panels themselves. The formation of a Seismic Review Panel for the proposed LNG facility near Point Conception, California, by the California Public Utilities Commission (CPUC) appears to be a major step in the right direction. The formal hearings, testimony and cross-examination by lawyers common in other regulatory reviews were substantially replaced by workshops run by the Panel, which is composed of geoscientists and earthquake engineers. The scientists and engineers representing the applicant, intervenors and CPUC staff were then allowed to make presentations and were questioned by the Panel. The legal representatives of the parties could be present, but were not allowed to participate and no verbatim transcripts of the workshops were made, although some points were recorded at the discretion of the Panel. The Panel made its report to the CPUC and, subsequently, cross-examination of the Panel was allowed and rebuttal testimony was filed, thereby preserving due process. This alternative procedure should be watched closely by those engineers and scientists concerned about settling the technical issues of major, regulated projects in a better manner than is now usually the case. See Ref. 13 for a description of this review procedure.

Figure 36. Multistory, steel frame building under construction in Los Angeles. The design criteria for this structure were based on estimated ground motions that might be generated on faults in the general vicinity. These included an $M_s = 8+$ on the San Andreas fault 35 miles distant and also included smaller earthquakes on closer faults. The dynamic response of the structure to these assumed ground motions was calculated on a digital computer, and shear forces, overturning moments, etc., were evaluated.

Conclusions

The project engineer and his staff have the basic responsibility for setting and implementing earthquake design criteria and obtaining any necessary approvals by regulatory bodies. In doing this, they should keep in mind that the purpose of the criteria is to specify the desired performance of the structure or facility under future conditions. Because it is not possible to prove that hypothetical events will not occur, it is not possible to formulate design criteria that ensure a zero probability of failure; the term "earthquake-proof" is to be avoided in recognition of this fact. However, some earthquakes are much more likely than others, and the project engineer should expect the recommendations of the geological, seismological and earthquake engineering consultants to include explicit, quantitative information about the likelihood of the various events and ground shaking they are recommending for consideration in setting the design criteria.

It has to be recognized that the project engineer cannot be an expert in all the fields of geology, seismology and earthquake engineering and therefore must rely upon consultants and upon his staff; however, it is essential that the project engineer know the right questions to ask. To assist this process, the following examples of questions are included here:

1. What active faults are located within 50 miles of the site; particularly, what faults are close to the site, and in what sense (recurrence rate, time of last rupture, etc.) are they active?

2. What significant earthquakes have occurred within 50 miles of the site? What were their characteristics?

3. What is the estimated frequency of occurrence of future earthquakes of various magnitudes in the general vicinity of the site?

4. What is the estimated intensity of ground shaking at the site that will be exceeded once per N years? (N may be one or

more of the following: 50, 100, 200, 1,000, 10,000 or more, depending on the data and the nature of the facility.)

5. What accelerograms, response spectra, or average spectra are representative of the ground motions, in terms of intensity, duration, and frequency content?

6. What would be the consequences to the structures and facilites to be designed of various degrees of overstressing and straining beyond the elastic limits? What are the requirements of safety on this point?

7. What would be an acceptable level of damage as balanced against probability of occurrence? (This is a question for the owner and any regulatory bodies involved.)

8. What ductility capability should the structure have, as balanced against the cost of providing it?

9. In view of the foregoing, what design spectra should be used; what design values of damping should be used; and what allowable stresses and strains should be used?

10. What resistive capability will the use of the design spectra, the design damping, and the allowable stresses and strains actually provide when the facility or structure is completed?

Because of the difficulty of the questions, completely satisfactory answers are not likely to be forthcoming, but an awareness of these questions and their answers will enable those responsible for the design of major projects to be in a better position to make the necessary technical decisions correctly and to guide the project through to a successful conclusion.

Appendix A
Two Case Studies in Reading and
Interpreting Earthquake Response

A detailed discussion of the measured response of two buildings to strong ground shaking is presented here. The first example is that of a 15-story steel frame structure that received only nonstructural damage during the San Fernando earthquake of 1971. The records for this building are examined and then used to calculate the base shear, base moment and maximum deflection experienced during the earthquake by means of simple, hand calculations. The results are compared to values used in the design and to the results of a more detailed, computer-aided research study.

In the second case study, the subject is the Imperial County Services Building, a 6-story reinforced concrete structure that was severely damaged during the earthquake of 1979. The records obtained in this building are the first made in a building sustaining major structural damage. In this example, no calculations are made; rather, the discussion is focused upon various details in the accelerograms that indicate the onset and propagation of the damage.

The two examples are followed by a brief presentation of the results of systematic studies of building response using computer-aided techniques.

Kajima International Building

Figure A–1 shows the Kajima International Building, which was strongly shaken in the San Fernando earthquake of February 9, 1971, but did not sustain any significant structural damage. The building is located in central Los Angeles, approximately 20 miles south of the center of energy release in the earthquake. The building, designed in 1966, consists of a 15-story tower, 66 x 96 feet in plan, partly surrounded by a three-story parking structure; the two parts of the building are separated by a seismic joint.

Figure A-1. The Kajima International Building in downtown Los Angeles. This steel-framed structure was strongly shaken during the San Fernando earthquake (Feb. 9, 1971). The basement, 8th floor and roof motions were recorded by strong-motion accelerographs.

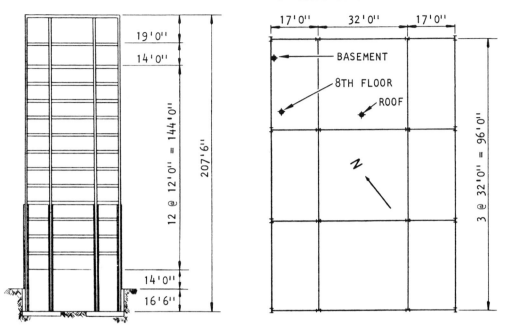

(a) *Profile*   (b) *Plan view*

Figure A-2. Structural configuration of the Kajima International Building. Earthquake motions are resisted by four frames in each direction. The locations of the accelerometers are indicated in the plan view.

The structural configuration of the tower is shown in Fig. A–2. A three-dimensional moment-resisting frame provides resistance to both lateral and vertical loads. There are four moment-resisting frames in both the transverse and longitudinal directions, and concrete encasement of the exterior columns of the frame for fire protection provides additional stiffness. Lightweight reinforced concrete floor slabs act as rigid diaphragms for horizontal motion. Precast concrete spandrels, 6 feet deep, comprise part of the exterior of the tower. The foundations consist of spread footings combined in pairs. The parking structure was separated from the tower structure by a separation joint, but there was evidence of pounding at the 3rd floor level where the separation was 2.5 inches.

Strong-motion accelerographs were installed on the basement, 8th floor and roof of the building at locations indicated in Fig. A–2. These instruments each provided two horizontal and one vertical record of the motion at the instrument site. We shall use the records from the Kajima building to illustrate the nature of responses of structures to earthquakes and to show how simple methods of analysis can be used to judge the significance of the motions. Many of the results presented are based on the calculations and interpretations of the late R. B. Matthiesen, in the draft report prepared by the Seismology Committee of the Structural Engineers Association of Southern California. Figure A–3 shows photocopies of the significant portions of the three records, which were obtained on AR–240 accelerographs. The important features of the accelerograms have been labeled on the basement record. The ½-second time marks allow periods of oscillations to be determined, and the notation about the sensitivity provides information which is required for converting the amplitude of the record into acceleration. In this case, all three instruments have a sensitivity of 7.6 cm/g. The records from the 8th floor and roof are marked at 8.15 and 16.5 seconds, and they show the N54°W component, which is the bottom record on each accelerogram and is used for the following analysis.

The simplest comparison to judge the level of response is to compare the maximum level of acceleration on the top floor, expressed as a fraction of gravity, to the design base shear coefficient, expressed as a fraction of the weight of the building. The maximum acceleration at the top of a building is a rough measure of the maximum dynamic base shear, typically being a factor of two or more greater, and the actual capacity of buildings is typically well in excess of the design base shear. Thus, if the peak roof acceleration is no more than about twice the design base shear, this indicates that, barring direct evidence to the contrary, the structural strength of the building has not been exceeded.

The Kajima building was designed to meet the 1961 Los Angeles building code. For this code the zone factor Z is unity, the structural parameter K is 0.67, the period for design was estimated by $T = 0.1N$, with N the number of stories, and the factor $C = 0.05T^{-1/3}$ reduced to 0.0437. Thus, the design base shear factor is given by

$$\frac{ZKC}{W} = 0.029 \qquad (A\text{-}1)$$

The biggest peak on the horizontal roof accelerogram measured 2.5 cm peak-to-peak. From this and from the sensitivity of the instruments, the maximum roof acceleration is

$$\frac{A_{max}}{g} = \frac{2.5}{(7.6)(2)} = 0.164 \qquad (A\text{-}2)$$

Because the maximum roof acceleration is almost six times the design base shear factor, this simple analysis suggests that a more detailed examination is warranted. One such analysis is presented next; it includes the computation of the maximum base shear, base (overturning) moment and drift that the structure experienced during the earthquake. This is a simple hand calculation based directly on the measured response. It typically requires a few hours, assuming the masses attributable to the floor levels are available from the design calculations. The calculation for the N54°W direction is outlined below.

The first step in the procedure is to identify the period of the fundamental mode of vibration. This is the longest period of response shown by the structure during the earthquake and can

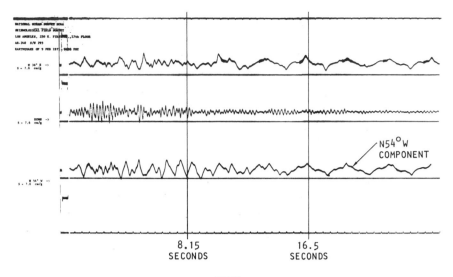

N54°W
COMPONENT

8.15
SECONDS

16.5
SECONDS

ROOF

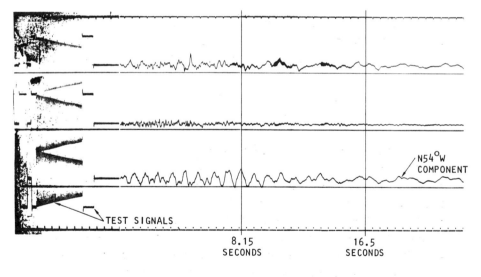

N54°W
COMPONENT

TEST SIGNALS

8.15
SECONDS

16.5
SECONDS

8TH FLOOR

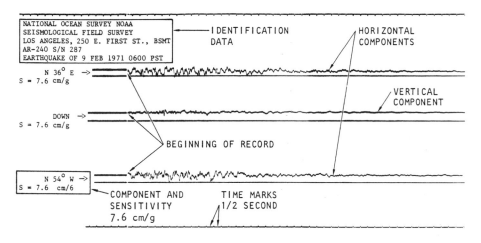

NATIONAL OCEAN SURVEY NOAA
SEISMOLOGICAL FIELD SURVEY
LOS ANGELES, 250 E. FIRST ST., BSMT
AR-240 S/N 287
EARTHQUAKE OF 9 FEB 1971 0600 PST

IDENTIFICATION
DATA

HORIZONTAL
COMPONENTS

N 36° E →
S = 7.6 cm/g

VERTICAL
COMPONENT

DOWN →
S = 7.6 cm/g

BEGINNING OF RECORD

N 54° W →
S = 7.6 cm/6

COMPONENT AND
SENSITIVITY
7.6 cm/g

TIME MARKS
1/2 SECOND

BASEMENT

Figure A-3. Records from the Kajima International Building during the San Fernando earthquake (Feb. 9, 1971). At time t = 16.5 sec, the fundamental mode is large, whereas the second mode dominates the response at t = 8.15 sec.

95

be identified on that basis, but it helps to have an idea of the period to reduce the possibility of confusion. A preliminary estimate of the fundamental period could be obtained from available pre-earthquake test measurements, from approximate formulae such as are used in design, or from earthquake response of similar buildings. It should be kept in mind, too, that the period of the building during strong earthquake motion can be appreciably larger than during small amplitude motions, by as much as a factor of two or three for response in which some structural members yield.

Sometimes the periods of the higher modes can be seen in the records and these modes can contribute substantially to the base shear and other features of the response. To estimate these periods it is useful to know that for framed structures the periods decrease approximately as the inverse of the odd integers, i.e.,

$$T_2 \approx \frac{1}{3} T_1 \qquad\qquad T_3 \approx \frac{1}{5} T_1 \qquad\qquad (A\text{-}3)$$

The decrease in periods for shear-wall structures is more rapid, but, because of the effects of shearing deformations and openings in the walls, they will not decrease as fast as a cantilevered bending beam for which

$$T_2 \approx \frac{1}{6} T_1 \qquad\qquad T_3 \approx \frac{1}{18} T_1 \qquad\qquad (A\text{-}4)$$

The calculations of overall measures of response like base shear and base moment also require some knowledge of the mode shape. Fortunately, the calculation is not sensitive to the details of the mode, and the mode shape can be estimated sufficiently well from the measured earthquake response and the known general character of mode shapes. The mode shapes in Fig. A–4 can be used if no other information is available.

For the Kajima building, the fundamental period in the lateral direction is known to be around 1.9 seconds on the basis of pre-earthquake measurements of wind response. The rule-of-thumb guide of $T = N/10$ suggests a comparable period, but

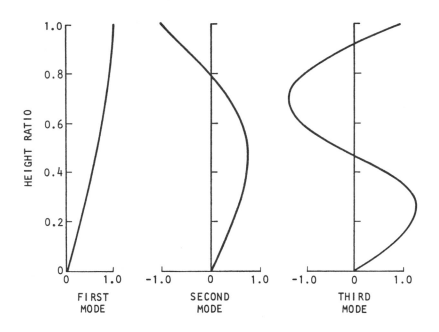

Figure A-4. Typical mode shapes for tall buildings. These mode shapes are representative of frame buildings of intermediate height. For taller buildings, the first mode shape approaches a straight line.

experience suggests an earthquake period larger than these numbers. Examination of the later part of the record on the roof (Fig. A-3) for periods of 2 seconds or more leads to the conclusion that the effective fundamental period during the earthquake was near 3 seconds. This result implies that the period of the 2nd mode of the structure is near 1 second and suggests that the roof response at 8 seconds into the record may reflect primarily the second mode. It is also seen that a large amplitude in the fundamental mode response occurs at 16.5 sec. into the record, and large amplitudes occur in the earlier, shorter period vibrations around 8.15 sec.

An enlarged view of the N54°W component of accelerations at the roof level and the 8th floor is shown in Fig. A-5 for the time period around 16.5 sec. After a smooth curve is drawn through the record, which has the effect of filtering out the response of the higher modes, a comparison shows that the two

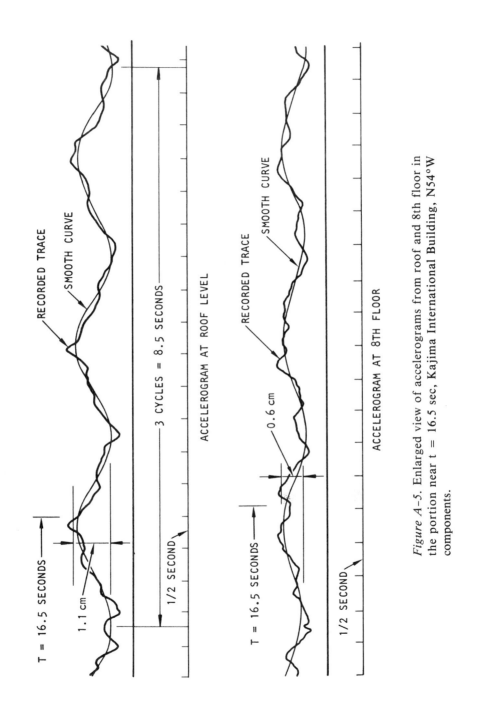

Figure A–5. Enlarged view of accelerograms from roof and 8th floor in the portion near t = 16.5 sec, Kajima International Building, N54°W components.

curves have the same period and phase, a necessary property of the fundamental mode. From the waveforms it is seen also that the period is 2.8 seconds and the amplitudes for floors 15 and 8 at 16.5 seconds are 1.1 cm and 0.6 cm, respectively. If these amplitudes are converted to accelerations by a calculation like Eq. A-2, the corresponding results are 0.072 g and 0.040 g. During this episode of response, the building is vibrating primarily in its fundamental mode, and the higher mode motion has been effectively removed by fitting a smooth curve through the response. Therefore, the acceleration ordinates found can be used to estimate the fundamental mode shape of the building, and the corresponding response of the building at each level can be calculated. The two accelerations are plotted against the height of the structure in Fig. A-6. From these two points a mode shape can be estimated, taking into account the fact that the mode shape must be zero at the base. The simplest interpretation is shown by the two straight lines. Also shown is a curved mode shape based on Fig. A-4. The differences are not significant and the straight lines were used to determine the accelerations shown at the right of the figure.

Envisioning the building vibrating in this mode shape with a maximum acceleration at the top of 0.072 g allows the maximum dynamic base shear and moment to be calculated from D'Alembert's principle: The desired force at each level is the mass at that level multiplied by its maximum acceleration. As indicated in Table A-1, this is conveniently done by multiplying the weight of each floor by the acceleration in g's: f = ma = w (a/g). The resulting force profile in column 5 then can be treated as if it were a problem in statics, and the shear at each level (column 6) and the moment at each level (column 7) can be calculated. The result shows that the structure, while vibrating in its fundamental mode around 16.5 seconds into the response, experienced a base shear of about 560 kips and a base moment of approximately 70,000 kip-ft. The neglected higher modes may increase the estimate for base shear, but would not be expected to contribute substantially to the base moment.

The results can next be compared to values used in the design. Table A-2 is a copy of calculations made by the Los Angeles Building Department. Such calculations are made during the

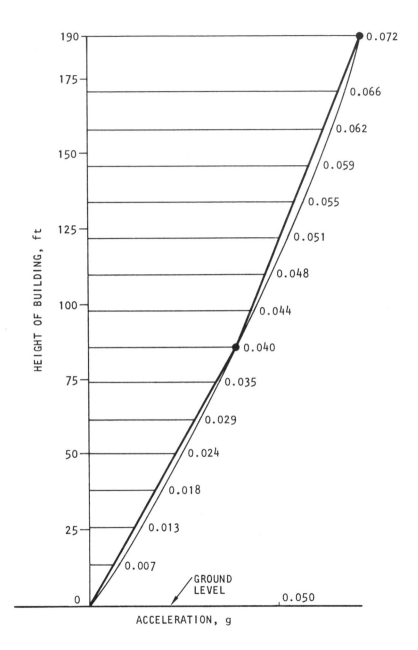

Figure A-6. Approximate first mode shapes determined by the measured response of the Kajima Building, N54°W components at t = 16.5 sec. The straight lines are used in the calculations; the smooth curve is based on Figure A-4. The circled values are from the records.

TABLE A-1. COMPUTED LATERAL FORCES AND OVERTURNING MOMENTS AT 16.5 SECONDS

Story	Height, ft.	Weight, kips	Acceleration, g	Force, kips	Shear, kips	Moment, kip-ft
Roof	190	800	.072	57.6		
15	171	1290	.066	85.1	57.6	1094
14	158	862	.062	53.5	142.7	2949
13	146	862	.059	50.8	196.2	5304
12	134	862	.055	47.4	247.0	8268
11	122	862	.051	44.0	294.4	11801
10	110	862	.048	41.4	338.4	15862
9	98	862	.044	37.9	379.8	20419
8	86	862	.040	34.5	417.7	25431
7	74	862	.035	30.2	452.2	30858
6	62	862	.029	25.0	482.4	36647
5	50	868	.024	20.8	507.4	42736
4	38	868	.018	15.6	528.2	49074
3	26	880	.013	11.5	543.8	55600
2	14	544	.007	3.8	555.3	62263
1	0	0	0		559.1	70090

Base Shear ≅ 560 kips
Base Moment ≅ 70,000 kip-ft

TABLE A-2. DESIGN LATERAL FORCES AND OVERTURNING MOMENTS
(Calculations by Los Angeles Building Department)

SEISMIC LATERAL FORCES AND OVERTURNING MOMENTS

Period used in computation	$T =$	1.50 sec
Base shear coefficient	$C =$	0.0437
Force factor	$K =$	0.67
Base moment coefficient	$J =$	0.3816
Concentrated force at top	$F(t) =$	0.00 kips
Base shear $V = KCW$	$V =$	380.68 kips
Overturning moment at base	$M =$	18749.73 ft-kips

Level	Height	Weight	Force	Shear	J@X	OTM	Cant. OTM
16	190.00	800.00	43.4	43.4	0.000	0.0	0.0
15	171.00	1290.00	63.0	106.4	0.832	686.6	824.8
14	158.00	862.00	38.9	145.3	0.737	1627.9	2208.3
13	146.00	862.00	35.9	181.3	0.662	2616.9	3952.0
12	134.00	862.00	33.0	214.3	0.599	3667.2	6127.2
11	122.00	862.00	30.0	244.3	0.545	4743.1	8698.2
10	110.00	862.00	27.1	271.4	0.502	5833.2	11629.6
9	98.00	862.00	24.1	295.5	0.466	6943.3	14886.0
8	86.00	862.00	21.2	316.7	0.439	8090.2	18432.0
7	74.00	862.00	18.2	334.9	0.418	9295.4	22232.0
6	62.00	862.00	15.3	350.2	0.403	10580.6	26250.7
5	50.00	868.00	12.4	362.5	0.393	11963.0	30452.5
4	38.00	868.00	9.4	372.0	0.387	13452.0	34803.0
3	26.00	880.00	6.5	378.5	0.383	15045.3	39266.6
2	14.00	544.00	2.2	380.7	0.382	16727.0	43808.7
1	0.00	0.00	0.0	380.7	0.382	18749.7	49138.1

Base Shear $\cong$ 381 kips
Base Moment $\cong$ 18,800 ft-kips

process of review of building plans prior to issuing a permit for construction. Most of the symbols in Table A–2 refer to well-known factors in the building code. The factor J is the overturning reduction factor, since eliminated from U.S. codes. The base, or overturning, moment (OTM) is found by multiplying the moment deduced from the force profile (Cant. OTM) by the value of the J-factor at the level of the building. From this table it is seen that the code base shear is 381 kips. The base moment is 49,100 kip-ft., and the reduced base moment is 18,800 kip-ft. These values can be compared to the 560 kips and 70,000 kip-ft. found from the earthquake response 16.5 seconds into the record. The 560 kips of base shear experienced during the earthquake is approximately 50 percent greater than the value used in design. If the seismic base shear controlled the design of some members, and if we recall that the allowable stresses are increased by one-third for earthquake response and that nominal yield stresses for steel are less than average values, the comparison indicates that some members were stressed about to the point where yielding begins.

Analyses such as described here would normally be done by an engineer familiar with the design of the building; the engineer would know, therefore, the degree that seismic forces controlled the design of structural members. This point is important in comparing the reduced base moment used in the design, 18,800 kip-ft., to the value of 70,000 kip-ft. induced by the first mode at 16.5 seconds. The base moment is most important for the exterior columns in the lower part of the structure; these columns also take large dead load stresses. The fact that the base moment in the earthquake was almost four times the design value indicates serious overstressing if the design base moment was a significant factor in sizing these columns. On the other hand, if the design base moment was not an important factor in designing the columns, then the large base moment experienced in the earthquake may not have caused excessive stresses. The designer of the building is obviously in the best position to make a meaningful comparison of the design and earthquake-induced moments. As an aside, the comparison does show rather convincingly that reduction of the moments in the building by use of the J-factor was not consistant with actual earthquake response, and that the subsequent removal of this reduction from the building codes was a wise decision.

The response at 16.5 seconds is not the only large motion caused by the earthquake, and the response near 8 seconds may also be important. As mentioned earlier, the period seen in the response suggested that this portion of the record was dominated by the second mode. An enlarged view of the response near 8 seconds is shown in Fig. A–7. The vertical line marks 8.15 seconds into the record, and it is seen that at this time the roof and 8th floor have about the same amplitude but are accelerating in opposite directions. Because the second mode is expected to have a period near 1 second, whereas the third mode would have a period around 0.6 seconds, it is concluded that the predominant motion seen in Fig. A–7 is that of the second mode.

To estimate the base shears and moments from the record at 8.15 seconds, smoothed versions of the first and second mode response were drawn as indicated in the figures. The first mode response is drawn by joining the midpoints of the waves of shorter period, and the second mode response is superimposed upon the larger-period motions. The maximum peak-to-peak amplitude of the first mode response is about 0.4 cm at the roof and 0.22 cm at the 8th floor. These values indicate a first mode shape consistent with that of the response near 16.5 seconds. To determine the second mode, the estimate may have to take into account the offsetting effects of the first-mode response. If any effects of the first mode are ignored, and a calculation like Eq. A–2 is performed, the resulting accelerations are 0.14 g at the roof and 0.15 g at the 8th floor. The other extreme would be to reduce the second mode response by the full amplitude of the first mode. In this case the resulting accelerations are

$$A_r = \frac{2.2 - 0.4}{(7.6)(2)} = 0.12 \text{ g}$$

$$A_8 = \frac{2.5 - 0.22}{(7.6)(2)} = 0.15 \text{ g}$$

(A–5)

A close examination of the records in Fig. A–7 suggests that the second mode amplitudes should be reduced by numbers less

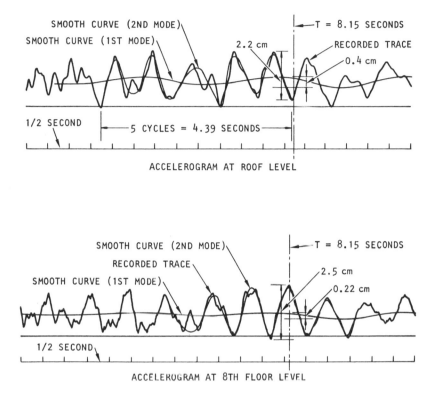

Figure A-7. Enlarged view of accelerograms from roof and 8th floor in the portion near t = 8.15 sec, Kajima International Building, N54°W components.

than the full amplitude of the first mode. The resulting differences in accelerations are insignificant in the present case, however; and the values in Eq. A–5 are used to calculate the base shears and moments.

Using the computed acceleration, the response of the two modes at 8.15 seconds can be constructed as shown in Fig. A–8. In this figure, the first mode is approximated by two straight lines, as in Fig. A–6, and the second mode is estimated from the measurements at the roof and 8th floor, and from Fig. A–4. These straight-line mode shapes determine the corresponding acceleration profiles and, since the masses are known, these can be turned into force profiles for static analyses by means of D'Alembert's principle. The resulting calculations are given in Tables A–3 and A–4 for the first and second modes, respectively. The first mode response leads to a maximum base shear of 200 kips and a maximum base moment of 25,000 kip-ft. The second mode response indicates a base shear of 550 kips and a base moment of 23,000 kip-ft. To find the combined response of the two modes, it is possible to deduce the phasing of the two modes from the records and use this information to determine combined values of base shear and moment. This refinement is not warranted in this calculation, however, and the combined responses at 8.15 seconds are reasonably estimated as indicated below:

$$\text{Base Shear} = \sqrt{(550)^2 + (200)^2} = 590 \text{ kips} \qquad \text{(A–6)}$$

$$\text{Base Moment} = \sqrt{(23,000)^2 + (25,000)^2} = 34,000 \text{ kip-ft.}$$

Alternatively, the worst combination yields

$$\text{Base Shear} \le 750 \text{ kips} \qquad \text{(A–7)}$$

$$\text{Base Moment} \le 48,000 \text{ kip-ft.}$$

The numbers in Eqs. A–6 and A–7 can be compared to the corresponding results at 16.5 seconds and to the design values. It is seen that the base shear in the earthquake response is greater at 8.15 seconds and the base moment is larger at 16.5 seconds. The base shear at 8.15 seconds is 1½ to 2 times the design value of

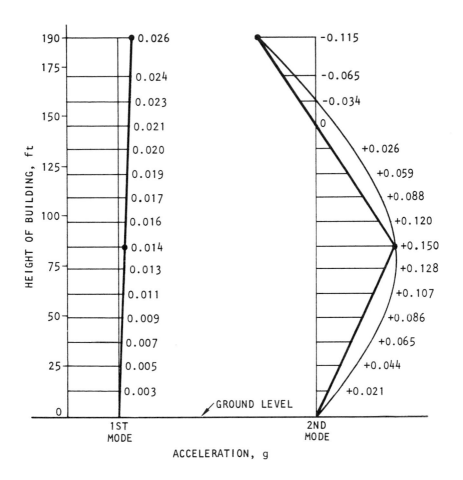

Figure A-8. Approximate mode shapes determined from the measured response of the Kajima International Building, N54°W components, at t = 8.15 sec. The straight line mode shapes are used in the calculations; the curved second mode shape is based on Figure A-4.

TABLE A-3. COMPUTED LATERAL FORCES AND OVERTURNING MOMENTS AT 8.15 SECONDS— 1ST MODE RESPONSE

Story	Height, ft.	Weight, kips	Acceleration, g	Force, kips	Shear, kips	Moment, kip-ft
Roof	190	800	.026	20.8		
15	171	1290	.024	30.9	20.8	395.2
14	158	862	.023	19.8	51.7	1067.3
13	146	862	.021	18.1	71.5	1925.3
12	134	862	.020	17.2	89.6	3000.5
11	122	862	.019	16.4	106.8	4282.1
10	110	862	.017	14.7	123.2	5760.5
9	98	862	.016	13.8	137.9	7415.3
8	86	862	.014	12.1	151.7	9235.7
7	74	862	.013	11.2	163.8	11201.3
6	62	862	.011	9.5	175.0	13301.3
5	50	868	.009	7.8	184.5	15515.3
4	38	868	.007	6.0	192.3	17822.9
3	26	880	.005	4.4	198.3	20202.5
2	14	544	.003	1.6	202.7	22634.9
1	0	0	0		204.3	25495.1

Base Shear $\cong$ 200 kips
Base Moment $\cong$ 25,000 kip-ft

TABLE A-4. COMPUTED LATERAL FORCES AND OVERTURNING MOMENTS AT 8.15 SECONDS— 2ND MODE RESPONSE

Story	Height, ft.	Weight, kips	Acceleration, g	Force, kips	Shear, kips	Moment, kip-ft
Roof	190	800	−0.115	−92.0		
15	171	1290	−0.065	−83.8	−92.0	−1748.0
14	158	862	−0.034	−29.3	−175.8	−4033.4
13	146	862	0	0	−205.1	−6494.6
12	134	862	+ 0.026	22.4	−205.1	−8958.8
11	122	862	+ 0.059	50.8	−182.7	−11148.2
10	110	862	+ 0.088	75.9	−131.9	−12731.0
9	98	862	+ 0.120	103.4	−56.0	−13403.0
8	86	862	+ 0.150	129.3	47.4	−12834.2
7	74	862	+ 0.128	110.3	176.7	−10731.8
6	62	862	+ 0.107	92.2	287.0	−7269.8
5	50	868	+ 0.086	74.6	379.2	−2719.4
4	38	868	+ 0.065	56.4	453.8	2726.2
3	26	880	+ 0.044	38.7	500.2	8728.6
2	14	544	+ 0.021	11.4	538.9	15195.4
1	0	0	0		550.3	22899.6

Base Shear ≅ 550 kips
Base Moment ≅ 23,000 kip-ft

381 kips, suggesting that some members may have gone into yield, depending on the extent the seismic base shear controlled the design.

The allowable drift, or interstory deflection, is a factor which is often very significant in the design of tall, steel-framed buildings. The recommended value of maximum allowable drift in the SEAOC *Commentary* (Ref. 9) is 0.005 h, where h is the interstory height. For the Kajima building, this implies a deflection of about 11.4 in. at the roof level. The allowable drift used in the design, however, was 0.0025 h, or 5.7 in. deflection at the roof. The maximum deflection at the roof during the earthquake can be estimated from the accelerogram by converting acceleration to displacement. At 16.5 seconds when the fundamental mode, which dominates the deflection, is largest and with the assumption that the acceleration is approximately sinusoidal, that is,

$$A = A_{max} \sin \frac{2\pi t}{T_1} \qquad \text{(A–8)}$$

the maximum deflection d is given by

$$d = T_1^2 \frac{A_{max}}{4\pi^2} \qquad \text{(A–9)}$$

With $A_{max} = 0.072$ g., this produces an estimated maximum roof displacement of 5.6 in. during the earthquake, indicating that the drifts in the building were essentially equal to the design values.

The design engineer is, of course, in the best position to judge the significance of the results of these simple analyses, but the fact that the base shears and moments from the earthquake response are significantly larger than the values used in design, and the fact that the drift reached the design value, do indicate the possibility of significant overstressing. If study of the design calculations do not show that exceedance of the seismic design stresses by this amount is permissible because of other controlling factors, it is recommended that a more detailed analysis of

110

the response of the building be made, using computer methods and the measured ground motion. It would also be prudent to make a careful visual inspection of the structure, including the uncovering of highly-stressed members or joints.

Detailed analyses were, in fact, done for the Kajima building. The results of the study by the Muto Institute included the following: Maximum base shear 860 kips, maximum base moment 90,000 kip-ft., and maximum roof displacement, 5.9 in. The analysis also indicated that there was slight yielding in some structural members, but no significant structural damage.

The results of the computer study are slightly different from those found by the simpler hand calculation presented above, but are not necessarily more accurate as far as the base shear, base moment and maximum displacement are concerned. It was necessary in the computer study to assume specific values of damping in the modes and to assume that modal periods did not change with time. The different assumptions required for the two sets of analyses could account for the different results. The principal advantage of the computer study is that estimates of responses for individual structural members can be found, which is information not furnished by the simple calculation presented above.

A notable feature of the records is the occurrence of narrow pulses later in the record when the fundamental mode reaches its maximum response. As can be seen in the roof record in Fig. A–3, the larger responses are accompanied by a pulse at the points of maximum amplitude. The phasing of the pulses with respect to the first mode rules out this being an effect of a higher mode. The pulses are in the direction of the acceleration of the first mode and therefore represent a sudden increase in the internal forces pushing the building back toward equilibrium. The pulses do not seem to be present in the records for the 8th floor. There are two principal candidates for the origin of the pulses: pounding of the tower against the adjacent parking structure, and a nonlinear stiffening effect provided by non-structural elements, most probably the precast concrete spandrels. Because the pulses are not obvious on the 8th floor records, it seems unlikely that pounding at the 3rd floor could have produced the pulses on the roof. It seems more probable

111

that joints of the spandrels closed up at the peak excursions of the building and this sudden increase in stiffness produced the acceleration pulses.

Imperial County Services Building

The previous example illustrates what can be learned from a straight-forward analysis of the records of a building that is strongly shaken but remains essentially undamaged structurally. The resistive capacity of structures goes beyond this level of response, of course. Although no records have yet been obtained from a building that collapsed from strong shaking, an excellent set of records was obtained from the heavily damaged Imperial County Services Building during the earthquake of October 15, 1979. The set of accelerogram traces is shown in Fig. A-9; these very informative records will be discussed below. The damage to the building is illustrated in Figs. A-10 and A-11. The earthquake resistance of the building was provided by shear walls in the transverse direction and by a moment-resistant frame in the longitudinal direction. The architectural configuration of the building led to a concentration of damage in the open first story. All of the beams and columns on this story were damaged, with the most severe failure shown in Fig. A-11.

The building had been subjected to ambient vibration tests before the earthquake, so its small amplitude periods of vibration were known (Ref. 8). These values help in interpreting the early, small amplitude, response. The 13 acceleration pickups in the building were located throughout the structure as indicated in the insert in Figure A-9. As indicated, the installation also included a free-field tri-axial instrument 340 feet east of the building. The reason the building was so well instrumented is that it had been chosen by the State of California's Strong-Motion Instrumentation Program for a comprehensive array.

The first shear waves arrived about 5 seconds after the instruments were triggered by the vertical component of the P-wave (trace 12). A look at the EW response, traces 4, 5 and 6, shows the portion of response between 1 and 2¾ seconds to have a period of about 0.3 seconds. This value, plus the phasing of the response at the three different levels, indicates that this is the second mode of response. (The first mode showed a period of 0.65 seconds in the ambient measurements.) The period of the motion changed markedly at about 2¾ seconds, at the same time that a short burst of high frequency motion appears on the records. This burst occurs, in fact, on all the traces, even those at the ground level, and coincides with very large peaks in the NS response (e.g. traces 1, 2 and 3) as well as the EW motion (trace 4). After 2¾ seconds, the EW motion in traces 4, 5 and 6 is more nearly in phase, particularly the roof and 4th floor motions, and the period has lengthened to nearly 1.6 seconds, implying nonlinear response. It is thought that the partial hinging of all the first-story columns occurred at 2¾ seconds, possibly triggered by the heavy loads experienced by the corner columns when the NS and EW responses peaked simultaneously. In the EW direction, this long period motion continues for the rest of the record, with the period lengthening further to nearly 2 seconds. The records are marked by occasional small bursts of very high frequency response, with a large, prolonged burst 7¼ seconds into the record. This large burst is again seen on all the records, including the ground level motions. On trace 9 the burst was so strong that the instrument failed to record all of the motion. It is also quite prominent on trace 3, and less so on traces 1 or 2. Traces 9 and 3 are directly above the line of collapsed columns, and it is believed that the response at 7¼ seconds records the failure of these columns. The bursts at 8¾ and 10¾ seconds may correspond to further settling of this end of the building.

The first mode period of NS response was found to be about 0.45 seconds in the ambient measurements. This period can be seen in the early parts of traces 1, 2 and 3 although these traces, and the second floor records (traces 7, 8 and 9) suggest the response up to about 2½ seconds is the combination of at least two modes. At about 2¾ seconds, a high frequency spike occurs in all the NS records, including ground level, but not in the free-field record. The spike is somewhat larger at the west end and center of the building than on the east end, in the records of the roof, second and ground floor levels. Because the spike appears to travel up the building, it may reflect something

113

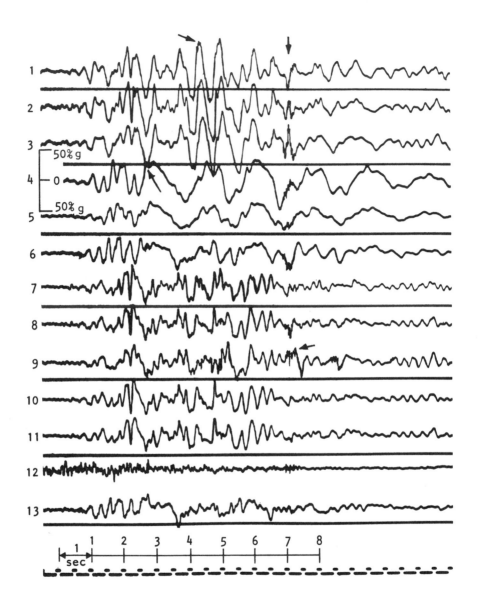

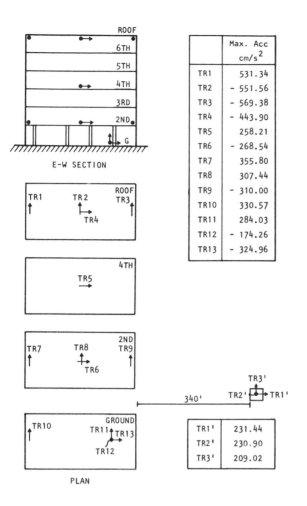

	Max. Acc cm/s^2
TR1	531.34
TR2	− 551.56
TR3	− 569.38
TR4	− 443.90
TR5	258.21
TR6	− 268.54
TR7	355.80
TR8	307.44
TR9	− 310.00
TR10	330.57
TR11	284.03
TR12	− 174.26
TR13	− 324.96

TR1'	231.44
TR2'	230.90
TR3'	209.02

Figure A-9. Accelerograms obtained from the Imperial County Services Building during the earthquake of October 15, 1979. The insert shows the location of the traces, which are arranged in descending numerical order. The free-field records are not shown. The insert also shows the peak accelerations from the traces. Time and amplitude scales have been added to the record, as well as four arrows indicating points discussed in the test. The records were obtained under the program operated by the California Office of Strong Motion Studies, Division of Mines and Geology.

115

Figure A-10. The Imperial County Services Building, looking north, photographed the day after the October 15, 1979 earthquake. At this distance, the only visible damage was the sagging of the easternmost bay on the right side of the photograph.

Figure A–11. Failed line of columns at the east end of the Imperial County Services Building. The upper photo shows all four columns as seen looking south. The lower photograph is of the most heavily damaged column on the southeast corner of the building. The failure of the columns occurred at the juncture between closely spaced ties below grade and the widely-spaced ties seen in the photographs. The photographs were taken the day after the earthquake.

117

happening in the foundation, for example, cracking of some piles at the pile cap. Another possibility is that the spike marks the observed failure (diagonal crack) of one of the two interior shear walls of the building, at the top of the open first story, although this possibility seems to require opposite directions on the spikes in the ground and second floor records. Later in the response, around 4 seconds, the NS roof motion shows a period of about ¾ of a second. These peaks, the largest in the response, give a maximum response acceleration of about 0.60 g.

Accelerometers 1 to 3 and 7 to 9 are situated to measure both torsion of the building and in-plane deformation of the floor slab. At the second floor level, traces 7, 8 and 9 tend to move together for the first 4 seconds or so. After 7 seconds, however, there are significant differences among the traces, with trace 9 being least like the other two. The records suggest approximately symmetric response up until the failure of the columns, with significant torsion thereafter, with the east end of the building moving more than the west end. At the roof, records 1, 2 and 3 are generally similar through about 5 seconds. There are enough differences at higher frequencies, however, to suggest torsional components in some of the higher modes. Also, the somewhat larger responses of trace 2 indicate the possibility of some in-plane bending of the roof slab. The records tend to show more differences in the later part of the motion; around 5½ seconds and 9 seconds are perhaps the two most prominent times. The later portion of the record may be showing some torsional response of the building, which at that time had become markedly asymmetric.

Other Studies of Building Response

Careful examinations of records from individual buildings, such as the two previous examples, can give insight into the nature of the response as well as quantitative information on the periods, base shears, base moments and deflections. To determine the effective damping of the structure or to estimate stresses in structural members requires more detailed modeling of the structure and more involved, computer-aided analyses.

The results of systematic studies of the response of a number

118

of buildings are summarized in Table A-5. These results were determined by applications of the techniques of system identification to the earthquake response of structures. By determining the parameters of a linear model of the structure that fit best the recorded response when excited by the recorded base motion, the methods give estimates of the effective period and damping of the structure. Some information about the mode shape is determined also. One of the better examples of the agreement between the recorded and calculated responses is given in Fig. A-12. The buildings listed in Table A-5 showed responses ranging from amplitudes less than 0.05 g to motions near 0.40 g; the latter were sometimes associated with minor structural damage. One of the important results seen in this data is the lengthening of the effective period of the buildings during the earthquake, in comparison with the pre-earthquake values. Even in the smallest earthquake response, elongations of the periods of 20 to 30% are common and lengthening of the period by a factor of two occurs for buildings shaken in the 0.20 g range. In both cases the buildings received no significant structural damages even though period changes of these amounts imply reductions in stiffness of 30 to 40% for the small motions and 75% for the larger motions. The fact that a building can lose, at least temporarily, about ¾ of its stiffness without structural damage indicates the complex relation that exists between the structural and nonstructural elements of the building. It also indicates strongly that design spectra should not be a rapidly varying function of the estimated period of a structure.

The last three buildings in Table A-5 experienced minor structural damage and their response was so nonlinear that it is difficult to analyze their motions satisfactorily using analyses based on linear models. Period elongations up to three times the pre-earthquake period were observed for these three buildings.

Table A-5 shows that for responses up to the point of minor structural damage the damping in buildings ranges from around 3% for the weaker motions to 7% for the stronger motions. These values give important guidance for selecting damping values for design, because damping values for design purposes cannot be calculated reliably. The higher values of damping shown for the last three buildings, which received minor

TABLE A–5. SUMMARY OF RESULTS FROM APPLICATION OF SYSTEM IDENTIFICATION TECHNIQUES TO EARTHQUAKE RESPONSE OF BUILDINGS (REF. 7)

Structure and Earthquake	Component	Stories	Construction	Miles From Pacoima Dam*	Max. Acc. (%g) Ground	Max. Acc. (%g) Response
JPL 180 - Borrego Mountain	S82E	9	Steel Frame	15	0.7	3.1
	S08W				0.7	2.3
- Lytle Creek	S82E				1.5	2.5
	S08W				2.4	3.7
- San Fernando	S82E				21	37
	S08W				14	21
Millikan - Lytle Creek	NS	9	R. C. Shearwall	19	1.9	5.4
	EW				1.9	3.5
- San Fernando	NS				20	31
	EW				18	34
1900 Avenue of Stars	N44E	27	Steel Frame	20	8	14
	S46E				8	11
Union Bank	S38W	39	Steel Frame	21	12	12
	N52W				15	20
KB Valley Center	S09W	18	Steel Frame	14	13	22
	S81E				14	22
Kajima	N36E	15	Steel Frame	21	9	19
	N54W				12	17
Sheraton-Universal	NS	19	R. C. Frame	15	16	11
	EW				15	18
Holiday Inn - Marengo	S52W	7	R. C. Frame	22	13	41
	N38W				12	23
Holiday Inn - Orion	NS	7	R. C. Frame	8	25	38
	EW				13	31
Bank of California	N11E	12	R. C. Frame	14	22	28
	N79W				15	24

*Taken as the center of energy release in the San Fernando earthquake.

**Response types: A - Small amplitude motions, excellent matches of data and calculations, close to vibration test periods.

| Pre-Eq. | Fundamental Period (Sec) | | | 1st Mode Damping (%) | | Response Type** |
	Post-Eq.	Eq.	Eq/Pre-Eq.	Eq.	Tests	
0.91		1.09	1.2	2.9		A
0.88		1.15	1.3	2.7		
0.91		1.02	1.12	4.7		A
0.88		1.13	1.3	3.5		
0.91	1.01	1.26	1.4	3.8		C
0.88	1.16	1.42	1.6	6.4		
0.53		0.52	0.98	2.9	1–2	A
0.69		0.71	1.03	2.2	0.7–1.7	
0.53	0.54	0.62	1.17	6.4		C
0.69	0.79	0.98	1.4	7.0		
3.3	3.6	4.37	1.3	4.4		A–B
3.3	3.6	4.24	1.3	2.2		
3.11	3.7	4.63	1.5	4.9	1.5	B–C
3.53	4.1	4.71	1.3	4.1	1.7	
2.18	2.37	3.30	1.5	8.6		B
1.94	2.27	3.05	1.6	6.3		
1.32	2.10	2.84	2.2	3.8		B
1.88	2.15	2.77	1.5	3.6		
1.22	1.4	1.98	1.6	7.3		B
1.26	1.5	2.24	1.8	6.2		
0.49	0.63	1.17	2.4	5.0(?)		D
0.53	0.64	1.06	2.0	17.8		
0.48	0.68	1.42	3.0	19.2		D
0.52	0.72	1.20	2.3	17.3		
(0.85)	1.70	2.35	2.8	12.1		D
(1.33)	1.60	3.01	2.3	10.0		

B - Moderate amplitude motions, good to excellent matches of data and calculations, periods changed from vibration tests.

C - Variation of equivalent linear parameters with time, strongest response matched by time-invariant modes of response.

D - Minor structural damage, limit of linear models of response.

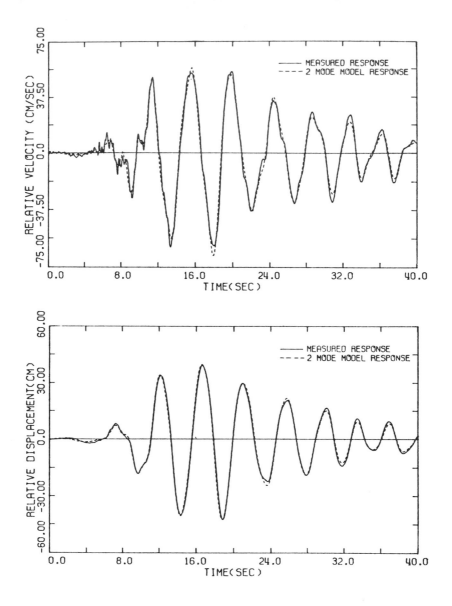

Figure A-12. Comparison of observed and calculated velocity and displacement for the N44°E component of the record obtained from the 27-story, steel-framed building at 1900 Avenue of the Stars in Los Angeles. The solid lines are from the measured responses during the San Fernando earthquake of February 9, 1971 and the dashed lines are the responses calculated from a two-mode model of the structure with properties determined by system identification. (Ref. 7)

122

structural damage, must be interpreted cautiously, as the assumption of linearity, which underlies the ideas of periods and damping, is breaking down at this level of response. The values of 10 to 20% damping for these buildings indicate only that if the strongest portion of the fundamental mode response of the building is modeled by a simple, linear oscillator, that oscillator must have a period and a damping value as indicated in Table A-5. These numbers give a descriptive understanding of the response, but seriously oversimplify the mechanics of the earthquake response at these amplitudes.

Appendix B
Earthquake Requirements in the
1982 Uniform Building Code

The Uniform Building Code (Ref. 14) is a form of earthquake design criteria in a broad sense. It is intended to apply to ordinary structures where special earthquake considerations are not cost effective. For critical projects, such as high-rise buildings, dams, offshore platforms, longspan bridges, power plants, major industrial facilities, etc., special earthquake considerations are advisable. The code is reproduced here as an example of design criteria that specify how structures are to be designed to resist earthquake forces. Because the code is a legal document that sets minimum requirements for earthquake resistance, its format is different than the earthquake design criteria for a nuclear power plant or for an offshore drilling platform; however, it can be seen that the concepts of design spectrum, ductility, etc., are reflected in the code even if not spelled out specifically. The code can be said to be a rather crude form of design criteria which does not consider such things as the different damping that different structures may have, etc., so that the actual resistance to ground shaking can be appreciably different for different structures, depending upon the engineering judgment used.

The sections of the code dealing with concrete, steel and wood are not reproduced here.

Earthquake Regulations

Sec. 2312. (a) **General.** Every building or structure and every portion thereof shall be designed and constructed to resist stresses produced by lateral forces as provided in this section. Stresses shall be calculated as the effect of a force applied horizontally at each floor or roof level above the base. The force shall be assumed to come from any horizontal direction.

Structural concepts other than set forth in this section may be approved by the building official when evidence is submitted showing that equivalent ductility and energy absorption are provided.

Where prescribed wind loads produce higher stresses, such loads shall be used in lieu of the loads resulting from earthquake forces.

(b) **Definitions.** The following definitions apply only to the provisions of this section:

BASE is the level at which the earthquake motions are considered to be imparted to the structure or the level at which the structure as a dynamic vibrator is supported.

BOX SYSTEM is a structural system without a complete vertical load-carrying space frame. In this system the required lateral forces are resisted by shear walls or braced frames as hereinafter defined.

BRACED FRAME is a truss system or its equivalent which is provided to resist lateral forces in the frame system and in which the members are subjected primarily to axial stresses.

DUCTILE MOMENT-RESISTING SPACE FRAME is a moment-resisting space frame complying with the requirements for a ductile moment-resisting space frame as given in Section 2312 (j).

ESSENTIAL FACILITIES—See Section 2312 (k).

LATERAL FORCE-RESISTING SYSTEM is that part of the structural system assigned to resist the lateral forces prescribed in Section 2312 (d).

MOMENT-RESISTING SPACE FRAME is a vertical load-carrying space frame in which the members and joints are capable of resisting forces primarily by flexure.

SHEAR WALL is a wall designed to resist lateral forces parallel to the wall.

SPACE FRAME is a three-dimensional structural system without bearing walls, composed of interconnected members laterally supported so as to function as a complete self-contained unit with or without the aid of horizontal diaphragms or floor-bracing systems.

VERTICAL LOAD-CARRYING SPACE FRAME is a space frame designed to carry all vertical loads.

(c) **Symbols and Notations.** The following symbols and notations apply only to the provisions of this section:

C = Numerical coefficient as specified in Section 2312 (d).

C_p = Numerical coefficient as specified in Section 2312 (g) and as set forth in Table No. 23-J.

D = The dimension of the structure, in feet, in a direction parallel to the applied forces.

δ_i = Deflection at level i relative to the base, due to applied lateral forces, Σf_i, for use in Formula (12-3).

$F_i F_n F_x$ = Lateral force applied to level i, n or x, respectively.

F_p = Lateral forces on a part of the structure and in the direction under consideration.

F_t = That portion of V considered concentrated at the top of the structure in addition to F_n.

f_i = Distributed portion of a total lateral force at level i for use in Formula (12-3).

g = Acceleration due to gravity.

$h_i h_n h_x$ = Height in feet above the base to level i, n or x respectively.

I = Occupancy Importance Factor as set forth in Table No. 23-K.

K = Numerical coefficient as set forth in Table No. 23-I.

Level i

l = Level of the structure referred to by the subscript i.

i = 1 designates the first level above the base.

Level n = That level which is uppermost in the main portion of the structure.

Level x = That level which is under design consideration.

x = 1 designates the first level above the base.

N = The total number of stories above the base to level n.

S = Numerical coefficient for site-structure resonance.

T = Fundamental elastic period of vibration of the building or structure in seconds in the direction under consideration.

T_s = Characteristic site period.

V = The total lateral force or shear at the base.

W = The total dead load as defined in Section 2302 including the partition loading specified in Section 2304 (d) where applicable.

EXCEPTION: W shall be equal to the total dead load plus 25 percent of the floor live load in storage and warehouse occupancies. Where the design snow load is 30 psf or less, no part need be included in the value of W. Where the snow load is greater than 30 psf, the snow load shall be included; however, where the snow load duration warrants, the building official may allow the snow load to be reduced up to 75 percent.

$w_i w_x$ = That portion of W which is located at or is assigned to level i or x respectively.

W_p = The weight of a portion of a structure or nonstructural component.

Z = Numerical coefficient dependent upon the zone as determined by Figures No. 1, No. 2 and No. 3 in this chapter. For locations in Zone No. 1, $Z = \frac{3}{16}$. For locations in Zone No. 2, $Z = \frac{3}{8}$. For locations in Zone No. 3, $Z = \frac{3}{4}$. For locations in Zone No. 4, $Z = 1$.

(d) Minimum Earthquake Forces for Structures. Except as provided in Section 2312 (g) and (i), every structure shall be designed and constructed to resist minimum total lateral seismic forces assumed to act nonconcurrently in the direction of each of the main axes of the structure in accordance with the following formula:

$$V = ZIKCSW \dots\dots\dots\dots (12\text{-}1)$$

The value of K shall be not less than that set forth in Table No. 23-I. The value of C and S are as indicated hereafter except that the product of CS need not exceed 0.14.

The value of C shall be determined in accordance with the following formula:

$$C = \frac{1}{15\sqrt{T}} \dots\dots\dots\dots (12\text{-}2)$$

The value of C need not exceed 0.12.

The period T shall be established using the structural properties and deformational characteristics of the resisting elements in a properly substantiated analysis such as the following formula:

$$T = 2\pi\sqrt{\left(\sum_{i=1}^{n} w_i \delta_i^2\right) \div \left(g \sum_{i=1}^{n} f_i \delta_i\right)} \dots\dots\dots\dots (12\text{-}3)$$

where the values of f_i represent any lateral force distributed approximately in accordance with the principles of Formulas (12-5), (12-6) and (12-7) or any other rational distribution. The elastic deflections, δ_i, shall be calculated using the applied lateral forces, f_i.

In the absence of a determination as indicated above, the value of T for buildings may be determined by the following formula:

$$T = \frac{0.05h_n}{\sqrt{D}} \quad\dots\dots\dots\dots\dots\dots\dots\dots \text{(12-3A)}$$

Or in buildings in which the lateral force-resisting system consists of ductile moment-resisting space frames capable of resisting 100 percent of the required lateral forces and such system is not enclosed by or adjoined by more rigid elements tending to prevent the frame from resisting lateral forces:

$$T = 0.10N \dots\dots\dots\dots\dots\dots\dots\dots \text{(12-3B)}$$

The value of S shall be determined by the following formulas, but shall be not less than 1.0:

$$\text{for } T/T_s = 1.0 \text{ or less} \quad S = 1.0 + \frac{T}{T_s} - 0.5\left[\frac{T}{T_s}\right]^2 \dots\dots\dots \text{(12-4)}$$

$$\text{for } T/T_s \text{ greater than 1.0 or less} \quad S = 1.2 + 0.6\frac{T}{T_s} - 0.3\left[\frac{T}{T_s}\right]^2 \dots \text{(12-4A)}$$

WHERE:

T in Formulas (12-4) and (12-4A) shall be established by a properly substantiated analysis but T shall be not less than 0.3 second.

The range of values of T_s may be established from properly substantiated geotechnical data, in accordance with U.B.C. Standard No. 23-1, except that T_s shall not be taken as less than 0.5 second nor more than 2.5 seconds. T_s shall be that value within the range of site periods, as determined above, that is nearest to T.

When T_s is not properly established, the value of S shall be 1.5.

> **EXCEPTION:** Where T has been established by a properly substantiated analysis and exceeds 2.5 seconds, the value of S may be determined by assuming a value of 2.5 seconds for T_s.

(e) **Distribution of Lateral Forces.** 1. **Structures having regular shapes or framing systems.** The total lateral force V shall be distributed over the height of the structure in accordance with Formulas (12-5), (12-6) and (12-7).

$$V = F_t + \sum_{i=1}^{n} F_i \quad\dots\dots\dots\dots\dots\dots \text{(12-5)}$$

The concentrated force at the top shall be determined according to the following formula:

$$F_t = 0.07TV \dots\dots\dots\dots\dots\dots\dots \text{(12-6)}$$

F_t need not exceed $0.25V$ and may be considered as 0 where T is 0.7 second or less. The remaining portion of the total base shear V shall be distributed over the height of the structure including level n according to the following formula:

$$F_x = \frac{(V - F_t)\ w_x h_x}{\sum\limits_{i=1}^{n} w_i h_i} \quad \dots\dots\dots\dots\dots\dots\dots (12\text{-}7)$$

At each level designated as x, the force F_x shall be applied over the area of the building in accordance with the mass distribution on that level.

2. Setbacks. Buildings having setbacks wherein the plan dimension of the tower in each direction is at least 75 percent of the corresponding plan dimension of the lower part may be considered as uniform buildings without setbacks, provided other irregularities as defined in this section do not exist.

3. Structures having irregular shapes or framing systems. The distribution of the lateral forces in structures which have highly irregular shapes, large differences in lateral resistance or stiffness between adjacent stories, or other unusual structural features, shall be determined considering the dynamic characteristics of the structure.

4. Accidental torsion. In addition to the requirements of Section 2303 (b) 2, where the vertical resisting elements depend on diaphragm action for shear distribution at any level, the shear-resisting elements shall be capable of resisting a torsional moment assumed to be equivalent to the story shear acting with an eccentricity of not less than 5 percent of the maximum building dimension at that level.

(f) **Overturning.** At any level the incremental changes of the design overturning moment, in the story under consideration, shall be distributed to the various resisting elements in the same proportion as the distribution of the shears in the resisting system. Where other vertical members are provided which are capable of partially resisting the overturning moments, a redistribution may be made to these members if framing members of sufficient strength and stiffness to transmit the required loads are provided.

Where a vertical resisting element is discontinuous, the overturning moment carried by the lowest story of that element shall be carried down as loads to the foundation.

(g) **Lateral Force on Elements of Structures and Nonstructural Components.** Parts or portions of structures, nonstructural components and their anchorage to the main structural system shall be designed for lateral forces in accordance with the following formula:

$$F_p = ZIC_p W_p \quad \dots\dots\dots\dots\dots\dots\dots (12\text{-}8)$$

The values of C_p are set forth in Table No. 23-J. The value of the I coefficient shall be the value used for the building.

129

EXCEPTIONS: 1. The value of I for panel connectors shall be as given in Section 2312 (j) 3 C.

2. The value of I for anchorage of machinery and equipment required for life safety systems shall be 1.5.

The distribution of these forces shall be according to the gravity loads pertaining thereto.

For applicable forces on diaphragms and connections for exterior panels, refer to Sections 2312 (j) 2 C and 2312 (j) 3 C.

(h) **Drift and Building Separations.** Lateral deflections or drift of a story relative to its adjacent stories shall not exceed 0.005 times the story height unless it can be demonstrated that greater drift can be tolerated. The displacement calculated from the application of the required lateral forces shall be multiplied by $(1.0/K)$ to obtain the drift. The ratio $(1.0/K)$ shall be not less than 1.0.

All portions of structures shall be designed and constructed to act as an integral unit in resisting horizontal forces unless separated structurally by a distance sufficient to avoid contact under deflection from seismic action or wind forces.

(i) **Alternate Determination and Distribution of Seismic Forces.** Nothing in Section 2312 shall be deemed to prohibit the submission of properly substantiated technical data for establishing the lateral forces and distribution by dynamic analyses. In such analyses the dynamic characteristics of the structure must be considered.

(j) **Structural Systems. 1. Ductility requirements.** A. All buildings designed with a horizontal force factor $K = 0.67$ or 0.80 shall have ductile moment-resisting space frames.

B. Buildings more than 160 feet in height shall have ductile moment-resisting space frames capable of resisting not less than 25 percent of the required seismic forces for the structure as a whole.

EXCEPTION: Buildings more than 160 feet in height in Seismic Zones Nos. 1 and 2 may have concrete shear walls designed in accordance with Section 2627 or braced frames designed in conformance with Section 2312 (j) 1 G of this code in lieu of a ductile moment-resisting space frame, provided a K value of 1.00 or 1.33 is utilized in the design.

C. In Seismic Zones No. 2, No. 3 and No. 4 all concrete space frames required by design to be part of the lateral force-resisting system and all concrete frames located in the perimeter line of vertical support shall be ductile moment-resisting space frames.

EXCEPTION: Frames in the perimeter line of the vertical support of buildings designed with shear walls taking 100 percent of the design lateral forces need only conform with Section 2312 (j) 1 D.

D. In Seismic Zones No. 2, No. 3 and No. 4 all framing elements not required by design to be part of the lateral force-resisting system shall be investigated and shown to be adequate for vertical load-carrying capacity and induced moment due to $3/K$ times the distortions resulting from the code-required lateral forces. The rigidity of other elements shall be considered in accordance with Section 2303 (b) 1.

E. Moment-resisting space frames and ductile moment-resisting space frames may be enclosed by or adjoined by more rigid elements which would tend to prevent the space frame from resisting lateral forces where it can be shown that the action or failure of the more rigid elements will not impair the vertical and lateral load-resisting ability of the space frame.

F. Necessary ductility for a ductile moment-resisting space frame shall be provided by a frame of structural steel with moment-resisting connections (complying with Section 2722 for buildings in Seismic Zones No. 3 and No. 4 or Section 2723 for buildings in Seismic Zones No. 1 and No. 2) or by a reinforced concrete frame (complying with Section 2625 for buildings in Seismic Zones No. 3 and No. 4 or Section 2626 for buildings in Seismic Zones No. 1 and No. 2).

> **EXCEPTION:** Buildings with ductile moment-resisting space frames in Seismic Zones No. 1 and No. 2 having an importance factor I greater than 1.0 shall comply with Section 2625 or 2722.

G. In Seismic Zones No. 3 and No. 4 and for buildings having an importance factor I greater than 1.0 located in Seismic Zone No. 2, all members in braced frames shall be designed for 1.25 times the force determined in accordance with Section 2312 (d). Connections shall be designed to develop the full capacity of the members or shall be based on the above forces without the one-third increase usually permitted for stresses resulting from earthquake forces.

Braced frames in buildings shall be composed of axially loaded bracing members of A36, A441, A500 Grades B and C, A501, A572 (Grades 42, 45, 50 and 55) or A588 structural steel, or reinforced concrete members conforming to the requirements of Section 2627.

H. Reinforced concrete shear walls for all buildings shall conform to the requirements of Section 2627.

I. In structures where $K = 0.67$ and $K = 0.80$, the special ductility requirements for structural steel or reinforced concrete specified in Section 2312 (j) 1 F, shall apply to all structural elements below the base which are required to transmit to the foundation the forces resulting from lateral loads.

2. **Design requirements.** A. **Minor alterations.** Minor structural alterations may be made in existing buildings and other structures, but the resistance to lateral forces shall be not less than before such alterations were made, unless the building as altered meets the requirements of this section.

B. **Reinforced masonry or concrete.** All elements within structures located in Seismic Zones No. 2, No. 3 and No. 4 which are of masonry or concrete shall be reinforced so as to qualify as reinforced masonry or concrete under the provisions of Chapters 24 and 26. Principal reinforcement in masonry shall be spaced 2 feet maximum on center in buildings using a moment-resisting space frame.

C. **Diaphragms.** Floor and roof diaphragms and collectors shall be designed to resist the forces determined in accordance with the following formula:

$$F_{px} = \frac{\sum\limits_{i=x}^{n} F_i}{\sum\limits_{i=x}^{n} w_i} \, w_{px} \qquad \dots\dots\dots\dots\dots (12\text{-}9)$$

WHERE:

F_l = the lateral force applied to level l.

w_l = the portion of W at level l.

w_{px} = the weight of the diaphragm and the elements tributary thereto at level x, including 25 percent of the floor live load in storage and warehouse occupancies.

The force F_{px} determined from Formula (12-9) need not exceed $0.30ZIw_{px}$.

When the diaphragm is required to transfer lateral forces from the vertical resisting elements above the diaphragm to other vertical resisting elements below the diaphragm due to offsets in the placement of the elements or to changes in stiffness in the vertical elements, these forces shall be added to those determined from Formula (12-9).

However, in no case shall lateral force on the diaphragm be less than $0.14ZIw_{px}$.

Diaphragms supporting concrete or masonry walls shall have continuous ties between diaphragm chords to distribute, into the diaphragm, the anchorage forces specified in this chapter. Added chords may be used to form subdiaphragms to transmit the anchorage forces to the main cross ties. Diaphragm deformations shall be considered in the design of the supported walls. See Section 2312 (j) 3 A for special anchorage requirements of wood diaphragms.

3. **Special requirements. A. Wood diaphragms providing lateral support for concrete or masonry walls.** Where wood diaphragms are used to laterally support concrete or masonry walls the anchorage shall conform to Section 2310. In Zones No. 2, No. 3 and No. 4 anchorage shall not be accomplished by use of toenails or nails subjected to withdrawal; nor shall wood framing be used in cross-grain bending or cross-grain tension.

B. **Pile caps and caissons.** Individual pile caps and caissons of every building or structure shall be interconnected by ties, each of which can carry by tension and compression a minimum horizontal force equal to 10 percent of the larger pile cap or caisson loading, unless it can be demonstrated that equivalent restraint can be provided by other approved methods.

C. **Exterior elements.** Precast or prefabricated nonbearing, nonshear wall panels or similar elements which are attached to or enclose the exterior shall be designed to resist the forces determined from Formula (12-8) and shall accommodate movements of the structure resulting from lateral forces or temperature changes. The concrete panels or other similar elements shall be supported by means of cast-in-place concrete or mechanical connections and fasteners in accordance with the following provisions:

Connections and panel joints shall allow for a relative movement between stories of not less than two times story drift caused by wind or $(3.0/K)$ times the calculated elastic story displacement caused by required seismic forces, or $\frac{1}{2}$ inch, whichever is greater. Connections to permit movement in the plane of the panel for story drift shall be properly designed sliding connections using slotted or oversized holes or may be connections which permit movement by bending of steel or other connections providing equivalent sliding and ductility capacity.

Bodies of connectors shall have sufficient ductility and rotation capacity so as to preclude fracture of the concrete or brittle failures at or near welds.

The body of the connector shall be designed for one and one-third times the force determined by Formula (12-8). Fasteners attaching the connector to the panel or the structure such as bolts, inserts, welds, dowels, etc., shall be designed to ensure ductile behavior of the connector or shall be designed for four times the load determined from Formula (12-8).

Fasteners embedded in concrete shall be attached to or hooked around reinforcing steel or otherwise terminated so as to effectively transfer forces to the reinforcing steel.

The value of the coefficient I shall be 1.0 for the entire connector assembly in Formula (12-8).

(k) **Essential Facilities.** Essential facilities are those structures or buildings which must be safe and usable for emergency purposes after an earthquake in order to preserve the health and safety of the general public. Such facilities shall include but not be limited to:

1. Hospitals and other medical facilities having surgery or emergency treatment areas.
2. Fire and police stations.
3. Municipal government disaster operation and communication centers deemed to be vital in emergencies.

The design and detailing of equipment which must remain in place and be functional following a major earthquake shall be based upon the requirements of Section 2312 (g) and Table No. 23-J. In addition, their design and detailing shall consider effects induced by structure drifts of not less than $(2.0/K)$ times the story drift caused by required seismic forces nor less than the story drift caused by wind. Special consideration shall also be given to relative movements at separation joints.

(l) **Earthquake-recording Instrumentations.** For earthquake-recording instrumentations see Appendix, Section 2312 (l).

133

TABLE NO. 23-I—HORIZONTAL FORCE FACTOR *K* FOR BUILDINGS OR OTHER STRUCTURES[1]

TYPE OR ARRANGEMENT OF RESISTING ELEMENTS	VALUE[2] OF *K*
1. All building framing systems except as hereinafter classified	1.00
2. Buildings with a box system as specified in Section 2312 (b) **EXCEPTION:** Buildings not more than three stories in height with stud wall framing and using plywood horizontal diaphragms and plywood vertical shear panels for the lateral force system may use $K = 1.0$.	1.33
3. Buildings with a dual bracing system consisting of a ductile moment-resisting space frame and shear walls or braced frames using the following design criteria: a. The frames and shear walls or braced frames shall resist the total lateral force in accordance with their relative rigidities considering the interaction of the shear walls and frames b. The shear walls or braced frames acting independently of the ductile moment-resisting portions of the space frame shall resist the total required lateral forces c. The ductile moment-resisting space frame shall have the capacity to resist not less than 25 percent of the required lateral force	0.80
4. Buildings with a ductile moment-resisting space frame designed in accordance with the following criteria: The ductile moment-resisting space frame shall have the capacity to resist the total required lateral force	0.67
5. Elevated tanks plus full contents, on four or more cross-braced legs and not supported by a building	2.5[3]
6. Structures other than buildings and other than those set forth in Table No. 23-J	2.00

[1]Where wind load as specified in Section 2311 would produce higher stresses, this load shall be used in lieu of the loads resulting from earthquake forces.

[2]See Figures Nos. 1, 2 and 3 in this chapter and definition of *Z* as specified in Section 2312 (c).

[3]The minimum value of *KC* shall be 0.12 and the maximum value of *KC* need not exceed 0.25.

The tower shall be designed for an accidential torsion of 5 percent as specified in Section 2312 (e) 4. Elevated tanks which are supported by buildings or do not conform to type or arrangement of supporting elements as described above shall be designed in accordance with Section 2312 (g) using $C_p = .3$.

TABLE NO. 23-J—HORIZONTAL FORCE FACTOR C_p FOR ELEMENTS OF STRUCTURES AND NONSTRUCTURAL COMPONENTS

PART OR PORTION OF BUILDINGS	DIRECTION OF HORIZONTAL FORCE	VALUE OF C_p[1]
1. Exterior bearing and nonbearing walls, interior bearing walls and partitions, interior nonbearing walls and partitions—see also Section 2312 (j) 3 C. Masonry or concrete fences over 6 feet high	Normal to flat surface	0.3[6]
2. Cantilever elements: a. Parapets	Normal to flat surfaces	0.8
b. Chimneys or stacks	Any direction	
3. Exterior and interior ornamentations and appendages	Any direction	0.8
4. When connected to, part of, or housed within a building: a. Penthouses, anchorage and supports for chimneys, stacks and tanks, including contents b. Storage racks with upper storage level at more than 8 feet in height, plus contents c. All equipment or machinery	Any direction	0.3[2] [3]
5. Suspended ceiling framing systems (applies to Seismic Zones Nos. 2, 3 and 4 only)—see also Section 4701 (e)	Any direction	0.3[4] [7]
6. Connections for prefabricated structural elements other than walls, with force applied at center of gravity of assembly	Any direction	0.3[5]

[1]C_p for elements laterally self-supported only at the ground level may be two thirds of value shown.

[2]W_p for storage racks shall be the weight of the racks plus contents. The value of C_p for racks over two storage support levels in height shall be 0.24 for the levels below the top two levels. In lieu of the tabulated values steel storage racks may be designed in accordance with U.B.C. Standard No. 27-11.

Where a number of storage rack units are interconnected so that there are a minimum of four vertical elements in each direction on each column line designed to resist horizontal forces, the design coefficients may be as for a building with K values from Table No. 23-I, $CS = 0.2$ for use in the formula $V = ZIKCSW$ and W equal to the total dead load plus 50 percent of the rack-rated capacity. Where the design and rack configurations are in accordance with this paragraph, the design provisions in U.B.C. Standard No. 27-11 do not apply.

[3]For flexible and flexibly mounted equipment and machinery, the appropriate values of C_p shall be determined with consideration given to both the dynamic properties of the equipment and machinery and to the building or structure in which it is placed but shall be not less than the listed values. The design of the equipment and machinery and their anchorage is an integral part of the design and specification of such equipment and masonry.

For essential facilities and life safety systems, the design and detailing of equipment which must remain in place and be functional following a major earthquake shall consider drifts in accordance with Section 2312 (k).

[4]Ceiling weight shall include all light fixtures and other equipment which is laterally supported by the ceiling. For purposes of determining the lateral force, a ceiling weight of not less than 4 pounds per square foot shall be used.

[5]The force shall be resisted by positive anchorage and not by friction.

[6]See also Section 2309 (b) for minimum load and deflection criteria for interior partitions.

[7]Does not apply to ceilings constructed of lath and plaster or gypsum board screw or nail attached to suspended members that support a ceiling at one level extending from wall to wall.

TABLE NO. 23-K—VALUES FOR OCCUPANCY IMPORTANCE FACTOR I

TYPE OF OCCUPANCY	I
Essential facilities[1]	1.5
Any building where the primary occupancy is for assembly use for more than 300 persons (in one room)	1.25
All others	1.0

[1]See Section 2312 (k) for definition and additional requirements for essential facilities.

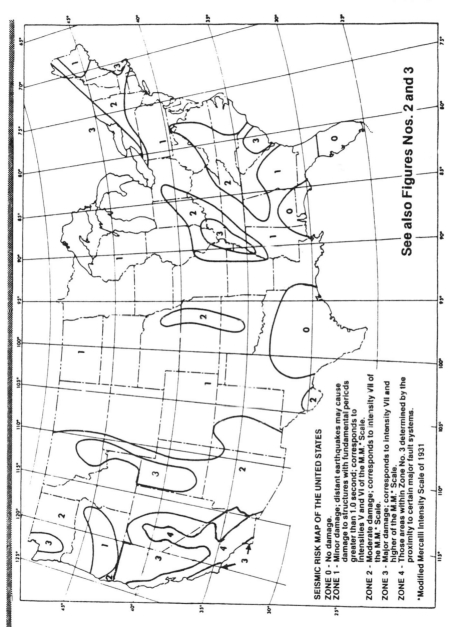

See also Figures Nos. 2 and 3

SEISMIC RISK MAP OF THE UNITED STATES

ZONE 0 - No damage.
ZONE 1 - Minor damage; distant earthquakes may cause damage to structures with fundamental periods greater than 1.0 second; corresponds to intensities V and VI of the M.M.* Scale.
ZONE 2 - Moderate damage; corresponds to intensity VII of the M.M.* Scale.
ZONE 3 - Major damage; corresponds to intensity VII and higher of the M.M.* Scale.
ZONE 4 - Those areas within Zone No. 3 determined by the proximity to certain major fault systems.

*Modified Mercalli Intensity Scale of 1931

FIGURE NO. 1—SEISMIC ZONE MAP OF THE UNITED STATES
For areas outside of the United States, see Appendix Chapter 23

REFERENCES

1. Allen, C. R. et al., "Relationship Between Seismicity and Geologic Structure in the Southern California Region," *Bull. Seis. Soc. Amer.*, 55:4, Aug. 1965, pp. 753–798.

2. Brandow, G. (coordinator) and D. L. Leeds (ed.), *Reconnaissance Report, Imperial County, California Earthquake, October 15, 1979*, Earthquake Eng. Res. Instit., Berkeley, CA, 194 pp.

3. Fox, F. L. and C. T. Spiker, "Intensity Rating of the Attica (N.Y.) Earthquake of August 12, 1929," *Earthquake Notes*, Eastern Section of the Seismological Soc. of Amer., 48:1 and 2, 1977.

4. Gutenberg, B. and C. F. Richter, *Seismicity of the Earth*, Hafner Pub. Co., New York, 1965.

5. Housner, G. W., "Behavior of Structures During Earthquakes," *Proc. Jnl. Eng. Mech. Div., ASCE*, EM4, Oct. 1959, pp. 109–129.

6. Jephcott, D. K. and D. E. Hudson, *The Performance of Public School Plants During the San Fernando Earthquake*, Earthquake Eng. Res. Lab., Calif. Instit. of Tech., Pasadena, 1974, 606 pp.

7. McVerry, G. H., *Frequency Domain Identification of Structural Models from Earthquake Records*, Rpt. No. 79–02, Earthquake Eng. Res. Lab., Calif. Instit. of Tech., Pasadena, 1979.

8. Pardoen, G. C., *Imperial County Services Building, Ambient Vibration Test Results*, Univ. of Canterbury, New Zealand, Civil Engineering Rpt. 79/14, 1979.

9. *Recommended Lateral Force Requirements and Commentary*, Seismology Committee, Structural Engineers Assoc. of California, 1980 edition.

10. Richter, C. F., *Elementary Seismology*, W. H. Freeman, San Francisco, 1958.

11. Rutenberg, A., P. C. Jennings and G. W. Housner, "The Response of Veterans Hospital Building 41 in the San Fernando Earthquake," *Proc. 7th World Conf. on Earthquake Eng.*, Istanbul, 1980.

12. Sackman, J. L. and J. M. Kelly, *Rational Design Methods for Light Equipment Subjected to Ground Motion*, Rpt. No. 78/19, Earthquake Eng. Res. Center, Univ. of Calif., Berkeley, 1978.

139

13. *Seismic Safety Review of the Proposed Liquified Natural Gas Facility, Little Cojo Bay, Santa Barbara County, California*, LNG Seismic Review Panel, Calif. Public Utilities Commission, Sacramento, Nov. 9, 1981.

14. *Uniform Building Code*, International Conf. of Building Officials, Whittier, CA, 1982.

15. U.S. Geological Survey, *United States Earthquakes*, Golden, Colo., annual publication.

16. U.S. Nuclear Regulatory Commission, *Regulatory Guide 1.60*, "Design Response Spectra for Seismic Design of Nuclear Power Plants," Washington, D.C., Dec. 1973, 6 pp.